Computer Engineering Step by Step

An Introduction to the Foundations of Computer Systems and Design

Julian Nash

Publisher email: info@tagvault.org

PREFACE

Welcome to *Computer Engineering Step by Step*! This book is your gateway into the dynamic and always-evolving field of computer engineering. Whether you're a student taking your first steps in this field, an aspiring engineer eager to explore the foundations, or simply a curious reader with a passion for technology, this book was written with you in mind.

Computer engineering sits at the intersection of hardware and software, bridging the physical components that make up computers with the abstract systems that bring them to life. It's an area of study that has transformed our world, touching every aspect of modern life — from the smartphones in our hands to the vast networks powering industries, healthcare, and even entertainment. While the field can seem intimidating at first, the beauty of computer engineering lies in its logical structure. Each concept builds on the last, forming a chain of understanding that unlocks countless possibilities.

The goal of this book is to guide you through that chain, one step at a time.

Why This Book?

Computer engineering can often feel overwhelming, especially for beginners. The sheer breadth of the field — spanning algorithms, hardware design, operating systems, memory systems, and beyond — can make it hard to know where to begin. That's why this book was designed to provide a structured, step-by-step journey through the essential topics, with each chapter focusing on core concepts that form the foundation of computer engineering.

This book takes a unique approach by balancing depth with accessibility. It's detailed enough to give you a strong grasp of technical topics but written in a clear and friendly language that welcomes readers of all levels. You don't need a background in mathematics or computer science to start your journey here. Instead, the chapters are crafted to introduce concepts in a logical order, ensuring that you can build on what you've learned as you move forward.

What You'll Learn

In *Computer Engineering Step by Step*, we'll explore both the "what" and the "why" of computer engineering. Starting with the foundational ideas — like binary systems, logic gates, and the architecture of computers — you'll gain a clear understanding of how computers process and store information. From there, we'll go into the building blocks of engineering, including digital circuit design, microprocessors, and embedded systems.

You'll also learn about critical topics like memory systems, operating systems, and programming. These are the backbone of modern computing, and understanding them will help you connect hardware with software. As you progress, you'll encounter practical areas like networking, databases, and cybersecurity—fields that are essential in today's interconnected world.

But we won't stop there. The book also covers exciting modern advancements like artificial intelligence, machine learning, and emerging technologies such as quantum computing and the Internet of Things (IoT). These topics are shaping the future of technology, and this book provides a high-level overview of how they fit into the broader context of computer engineering.

Who This Book Is For

This book is designed for a wide audience. If you're a beginner, you'll find an easy-to-follow introduction that explains complex topics in simple terms. If you're an aspiring computer engineer or a student, this book will reinforce your learning by providing a clear and structured roadmap through the key topics. Even professionals who want to revisit foundational concepts or explore emerging areas will find value in these pages.

A Step-by-Step Journey

The step-by-step structure of this book reflects the logical flow of computer engineering itself. Each chapter builds on the last, providing a seamless progression from one topic to the next. By the time you finish the book, you'll have a comprehensive understanding of how computers are designed, how they operate, and how they interact with the world around them.

At the end of the book, we've included an appendix with a glossary of terms and a timeline of computer engineering milestones. These resources are designed to enhance your learning experience and provide a quick reference when needed.

A Final Word

Computer engineering is more than just a technical field. It's a pursuit of creativity, problem-solving, and innovation. It's about designing systems that power modern life, developing algorithms that solve complex problems, and imagining the technologies of tomorrow. Whether you dream of building cutting-edge software, designing innovative hardware, or simply understanding the machines that shape our world, computer engineering is your gateway to limitless possibilities.

This book is your companion on this exciting journey. It's here to guide you, answer your questions, and inspire your curiosity. As you turn these pages, remember that every expert in computer engineering once started where you are now—with a desire to learn and explore.

Thank you for choosing *Computer Engineering Step by Step*. I hope this book provides you with the concepts, insights, and confidence to take your first steps into this fascinating field.

Let's take a look at our topical outline:

TOPICAL OUTLINE

Chapter 1: The Foundations of Computer Engineering
- The Evolution of Computer Engineering
- Understanding the Binary System
- Logic Gates and Boolean Algebra
- Overview of Computer Architecture
- Introduction to Algorithms
- Software vs. Hardware Engineering

Chapter 2: Computer Architecture
- Components of a Computer System
- Instruction Set Architectures (ISA)
- System Performance Metrics
- Parallel Processing and Multithreading

Chapter 3: Digital Logic and Circuit Design
- Combinational Logic Circuits
- Sequential Logic Circuits
- Finite State Machines
- Designing Simple Digital Systems

Chapter 4: Microprocessors and Embedded Systems
- Anatomy of a Microprocessor
- Microcontroller vs. Microprocessor
- Basics of Embedded Systems
- Role of Real-Time Operating Systems (RTOS)

Chapter 5: Memory Systems and Storage
- Memory Hierarchies: Cache, RAM, and Storage
- Primary vs. Secondary Storage
- Virtual Memory Concepts
- Solid-State Drives (SSD) vs. Hard Disk Drives (HDD)

Chapter 6: Operating Systems and System Software
- Functions and Components of Operating Systems
- Process Management and Scheduling
- Memory Management
- File Systems and Storage Management

Appendix
- Terms and Definitions
- Timeline of Computer Engineering

Afterword

TABLE OF CONTENTS

CHAPTER 1: THE FOUNDATIONS OF COMPUTER ENGINEERING

The Evolution of Computer Engineering

Computer engineering began long before the invention of modern computers. Its roots trace back to the earliest efforts to mechanize calculations and create systems for processing information. Understanding the evolution of computer engineering requires examining how machines, methods, and concepts have changed over time. Each development built upon the previous one, creating a field that now underpins nearly every aspect of modern life.

The story begins in antiquity, with devices like the abacus, a simple but effective tool for arithmetic operations. Used in various cultures for thousands of years, the abacus demonstrated humanity's desire to create tools that extend mental capacity. By standardizing and speeding up calculations, it became one of the earliest mechanical computing devices. However, true advances in engineering didn't begin until much later.

In the 17th century, mechanical calculators emerged, laying an important foundation. Wilhelm Schickard's "calculating clock" and Blaise Pascal's Pascaline were among the first attempts to automate arithmetic using gears and levers. These devices could perform basic addition and subtraction but were limited in scope. A significant leap came in the 19th century with Charles Babbage's designs for the **Analytical Engine**, a mechanical general-purpose computer. Although never fully constructed in his lifetime, Babbage's machine included key elements of modern computing, such as a control unit, memory, and input/output mechanisms. His collaborator Ada Lovelace wrote detailed notes on how the engine could be programmed, earning her recognition as the first computer programmer.

By the early 20th century, electromechanical devices began to replace purely mechanical systems. Machines like the **Zuse Z3** in Germany and IBM's **Harvard Mark I** combined electrical relays with mechanical components to execute programs. These early computers were slow and cumbersome but demonstrated the power of using electricity to control logic. The transition from mechanical to electromechanical systems signaled the start of a shift toward higher speeds and greater reliability.

The mid-20th century saw the **advent of electronic computers**, a transformative moment in computer engineering. Vacuum tubes replaced electromechanical relays, allowing for faster and more reliable computation. Machines like the **ENIAC** (Electronic Numerical Integrator and Computer) in the United States could perform thousands of calculations per second, a staggering improvement over earlier designs. However, vacuum tubes had limitations, including significant power consumption and a tendency to overheat.

The development of the **transistor** in 1947 by William Shockley, John Bardeen, and Walter Brattain at Bell Labs revolutionized computer engineering. Transistors were smaller, more efficient, and more reliable than vacuum tubes. This breakthrough marked the beginning of the **second generation of computers** and laid the groundwork for modern semiconductor technology. Transistors enabled engineers to design computers that were faster, cheaper, and far more compact, leading to the first commercial computers in the 1950s.

The next major milestone came with the invention of the **integrated circuit (IC)** in the late 1950s by Jack Kilby and Robert Noyce. By packing multiple transistors, resistors, and capacitors onto a single chip, ICs dramatically increased computational power while reducing the size and cost of computing devices. This innovation ushered in the **third generation of computers**, where mainframes became widely used in businesses, government, and research institutions.

One of the most transformative periods in computer engineering occurred in the 1970s with the development of the **microprocessor**. A microprocessor integrates a computer's central processing unit (CPU) onto a single silicon chip. Intel's **4004**, introduced in 1971, was the first commercially available microprocessor. Although it could only perform basic tasks, it demonstrated the feasibility of embedding a CPU in compact systems. Shortly after, the **Intel 8080** and other microprocessors enabled the creation of personal computers, starting a revolution in computing accessibility.

During this time, advances in **memory technology** also were critical. Early computers relied on magnetic drum and core memory, which were bulky and slow. The introduction of dynamic random-access memory (**DRAM**) in the 1960s and its subsequent refinement in the 1970s provided computers with faster and more reliable memory systems. DRAM chips stored more data in less space, enabling larger and more powerful computing systems.

By the 1980s, personal computers became widespread. Companies like IBM, Apple, and Microsoft were influential in popularizing home computing. The IBM PC, released in 1981, established a standard architecture that dominated the market for decades. At the same time, advancements in **operating systems** made computers more user-friendly. Systems like MS-DOS and later graphical user interfaces (GUIs), such as Apple's Macintosh System Software and Microsoft Windows, simplified how people interacted with computers, broadening their appeal beyond technical users.

The 1990s marked a shift from standalone machines to interconnected systems. The growth of the **internet** revolutionized computer engineering by emphasizing networking and distributed computing. Engineers developed faster network protocols, improved data transmission methods, and introduced concepts like cloud computing, which allowed for resource sharing on an unprecedented scale. This period also saw significant improvements in **processor design**, with companies like Intel and AMD introducing CPUs with multiple cores and increasingly complex architectures.

Another breakthrough came in the early 2000s with the rise of **mobile computing**. Smartphones, powered by processors like ARM-based chips, required computer engineers to focus on energy efficiency, miniaturization, and wireless communication. These challenges drove innovation in hardware and software design, leading to devices that were both powerful and portable. The integration of touchscreens, sensors, and mobile operating systems further expanded the boundaries of what computers could do.

Parallel to hardware advances, the field of **artificial intelligence (AI)** emerged as a defining aspect of modern computer engineering. While the concept of AI dates back to the mid-20th century, it wasn't until the development of powerful GPUs (graphics processing units) and neural networks in the 2010s that AI became practical on a large scale. Engineers leveraged these tools to create machine learning models capable of solving complex problems, such as image recognition, natural language processing, and autonomous driving.

Computer engineering today continues to evolve at a rapid pace. The development of **quantum computing**, for instance, challenges traditional notions of computation by leveraging the principles of quantum mechanics. While still in its infancy, quantum computers promise to solve problems that are intractable for classical systems, such as large-scale cryptography and optimization challenges.

Simultaneously, **edge computing** and the **Internet of Things (IoT)** are reshaping how and where data is processed. Instead of relying solely on centralized data centers, edge computing enables devices to process data locally, reducing latency and improving efficiency. This shift has implications for industries like healthcare, manufacturing, and transportation, where real-time decision-making is critical.

The field has also embraced **sustainability** as a key priority. Computer engineers now focus on reducing energy consumption in data centers, designing eco-friendly chips, and creating systems that minimize electronic waste. These efforts align with the broader societal push toward addressing climate change and conserving resources.

Computer engineering's evolution is a testament to human ingenuity and the relentless pursuit of better solutions. Each breakthrough, from the abacus to AI, reflects the creativity and dedication of engineers who transformed abstract ideas into practical technologies. These advancements continue to shape the modern world, influencing how we live, work, and communicate.

Today, the field stands on the cusp of new frontiers. Innovations like **neuromorphic computing**—which mimics the brain's structure and processes—offer exciting possibilities for the future. As computer engineers tackle increasingly complex challenges, they build on centuries of progress, demonstrating that the evolution of computer engineering is far from over.

Understanding the Binary System

The **binary system** forms the foundation of all digital computing. It uses just two digits, 0 and 1, to represent information. This simplicity is its greatest strength, as it aligns perfectly with the on/off nature of electronic components. Binary isn't just a coding system—it's a universal language that computers rely on to process, store, and transmit data.

At its core, the binary system is a **base-2 number system**, unlike the decimal system, which is base-10 and familiar to most humans. In decimal, each digit represents a power of ten. For example, the number 123 in decimal represents can be expressed as:

$$1 \times 10^2 + 2 \times 10^1 + 3 \times 10^0$$

In the binary system, each position represents a power of two. For instance, the binary number 1011 translates to:

$$1 \times 2^3 + 0 \times 2^2 + 1 \times 2^1 + 1 \times 2^0,$$

which equals 11 in decimal.

The binary system's reliance on two states—on and off—makes it highly suited for electronic circuits. **Transistors**, the fundamental components of modern electronics, act as switches that can either allow electricity to flow (representing 1) or block it (representing 0). This close alignment between binary digits and physical states allows computers to process and store data efficiently.

Binary arithmetic forms the backbone of computer operations. Adding two binary numbers follows the same principles as decimal addition but with simpler rules. For example:

$0 + 0 = 0$
$0 + 1 = 1$
$1 + 1 = 10$ (carry the 1).

These straightforward operations allow computers to execute complex calculations with speed and reliability.

Subtraction, multiplication, and division in binary work similarly to their decimal counterparts, but they require fewer symbols and simpler logic. This efficiency allows processors to perform millions or billions of calculations per second.

Computers don't just use binary for arithmetic. **Data representation** also relies on binary encoding. Characters, for example, are often stored using standards like **ASCII** (American Standard Code for Information Interchange). In ASCII, each character is represented by a unique 7- or 8-bit binary number. For instance, the letter "A" is 65 in decimal, or 1000001 in binary, while "a" is 97, or 1100001.

Beyond characters, binary is also used to represent **colors, sounds, and images**. Colors in digital images are often encoded in binary using schemes like RGB (Red, Green, Blue). Each color channel is assigned a binary value, with combinations producing millions of possible colors. Similarly, sound waves are converted into digital signals by sampling the wave at regular intervals and encoding the amplitude as binary values.

The concept of **binary logic** is another cornerstone of computer engineering. Binary logic uses **Boolean algebra**, a branch of mathematics that deals with true/false values, represented as 1 and 0 in computing. Boolean operations like AND, OR, and NOT are used in logic gates, the basic components of digital circuits. For example, an AND gate outputs 1 only if both inputs are 1, while an OR gate outputs 1 if at least one input is 1. These simple operations allow computers to make decisions and perform complex calculations.

Binary also facilitates **memory storage**. Inside a computer, memory is organized into a series of bits, with each bit storing a single binary digit. Groups of 8 bits, called bytes, are the smallest addressable units of memory in most systems. Larger groupings—like kilobytes, megabytes, gigabytes, and beyond—are all multiples of binary powers. For example, a kilobyte is traditionally 2^{10}, or 1,024 bytes, because binary powers naturally fit within the binary system's structure.

The use of binary extends to the **machine instructions** that control processors. Every operation a CPU performs, from adding numbers to accessing memory, is encoded in binary as **machine code**. For example, a processor might interpret the binary sequence 10110000 as a command to load data from a specific memory address. These instructions are executed at incredible speeds, enabling the complex tasks we take for granted.

Binary's impact isn't limited to hardware—it also underpins **software development**. High-level programming languages like Python or Java are eventually translated into binary instructions that a machine can understand. This process, known as **compilation**, ensures that human-readable code is converted into efficient binary commands optimized for execution by the processor.

One of the most fascinating aspects of binary is its **flexibility in representing non-integer values**. For example, fractions are stored using formats like **floating-point representation**. In this system, numbers are expressed as a combination of a significand, an exponent, and a base, all encoded in binary. This allows computers to handle very large or very small numbers, such as those used in scientific computations, with precision and efficiency.

Binary encoding also drives encryption and security systems. Data transmitted over the internet—like messages, files, or passwords—is converted into binary and then encrypted using complex algorithms. The encrypted binary data is secure and can only be decoded by authorized systems with the correct cryptographic keys. Without binary, the secure exchange of information that underpins modern digital communication would not be possible.

Networking protocols also rely heavily on binary systems. Internet addresses, for instance, are represented in binary. An **IPv4 address**, such as 192.168.0.1, is actually a 32-bit binary number split into four 8-bit segments. Similarly, data packets sent across networks include binary headers that dictate how the data is routed and processed.

Storage media, like hard drives and solid-state drives, encode data using binary patterns. On a hard drive, data is written by magnetizing microscopic areas to represent binary 1s and 0s. In solid-state drives, binary data is stored as charge states in flash memory cells. These physical representations of binary allow computers to save and retrieve vast amounts of information efficiently.

Even **error detection and correction** techniques rely on binary. When data is transmitted or stored, errors can occur due to electrical noise or hardware faults. Systems like **parity checks** or **Hamming codes** use additional binary bits to detect and correct errors, ensuring the reliability of digital communication and storage.

Binary is not limited to computation and storage; it also drives **decision-making processes** in systems like artificial intelligence (AI). AI models, particularly those based on neural networks, use binary weights and activations during training and inference. While the underlying algorithms may involve complex mathematics, binary operations ensure that computations are efficient and scalable.

Another critical application of binary is in **digital signal processing (DSP)**. Signals like audio or video, which are originally analog, must be converted into binary for processing by computers. This involves sampling the signal at regular intervals and quantizing the values into binary form. Once in binary, signals can be compressed, transmitted, or manipulated with incredible precision.

The binary system's efficiency also extends to the design of **finite state machines (FSMs)**, which are used in embedded systems, software applications, and even video games. FSMs rely on binary states to model and manage system behavior, making them ideal for applications where precise control and predictability are required.

One of the more modern uses of binary is in **quantum computing**, although it challenges some of binary's traditional limitations. While classical computers operate exclusively with 1s and 0s, quantum systems introduce **qubits**, which can represent a 0, a 1, or both simultaneously through a property called superposition. Even so, the principles of binary logic continue to guide the development of quantum algorithms.

The universality of binary ensures its continued relevance. As technology evolves, engineers will find new ways to use binary to solve problems, optimize systems, and expand the capabilities of computing.

Logic Gates and Boolean Algebra

Logic gates and **Boolean algebra** are fundamental to computer engineering. They form the backbone of digital circuit design, allowing computers to process binary data. Without these foundational tools, modern computing would be impossible. Boolean algebra provides the mathematical framework for logic, while logic gates implement these principles in hardware, enabling the flow of binary operations in a machine.

At the heart of Boolean algebra lies the idea that logical statements can be expressed mathematically using binary variables—values of 1 (true) or 0 (false). Developed in the mid-19th century by George Boole, Boolean algebra simplifies complex logical expressions into manageable forms. Its primary operations—AND, OR, and NOT— mirror basic decision-making processes. These operations are represented in equations using symbols: AND is typically written as a multiplication (AB), OR as addition (A + B), and NOT with an overline or prime (A' or ¬A).

Logic gates are physical implementations of Boolean operations using electronic components. These gates act as building blocks for all digital circuits, processing binary inputs to produce specific outputs. Each type of logic gate corresponds to a Boolean operation, enabling engineers to translate theoretical equations into functioning hardware. A **basic AND gate**, for example, takes two inputs and outputs 1 only if both inputs are 1. Conversely, an **OR gate** outputs 1 if at least one of its inputs is 1.

Truth tables are essential tools for understanding how logic gates work. They systematically list all possible input combinations and their corresponding outputs, ensuring no ambiguity in the gate's behavior. For instance, a truth table for an AND gate with two inputs, A and B, would show four possible combinations:

A = 0, B = 0 → Output: 0
A = 0, B = 1 → Output: 0
A = 1, B = 0 → Output: 0
A = 1, B = 1 → Output: 1

NOT gates are the simplest logic gates, inverting a single binary input. If the input is 0, the output is 1, and vice versa. This straightforward behavior becomes a critical element in constructing more complex operations, as inversion is often required to modify existing logic.

Beyond basic gates, there are **composite gates** that combine multiple operations. The **NAND gate** (NOT AND) outputs 0 only when all its inputs are 1. It's especially significant because it is a **universal gate**, meaning any other gate or Boolean function can be constructed using only NAND gates. Similarly, the **NOR gate** (NOT OR) is also universal and outputs 1 only when all its inputs are 0. Engineers frequently use these universal gates in design because they simplify manufacturing and reduce hardware complexity.

More specialized gates include the **XOR gate** (exclusive OR) and **XNOR gate** (exclusive NOR). The XOR gate outputs 1 only when its inputs differ, making it a critical component in operations like binary addition. The XNOR gate, in contrast, outputs 1 when the inputs are identical. These gates are often used in circuits requiring comparison or conditional execution, such as parity checks or error detection.

Combining multiple gates enables engineers to create **combinational circuits**, which produce outputs based solely on their current inputs. Common examples include **adders**, **multiplexers**, and **decoders**. An **adder circuit**, for instance, performs binary addition using a combination of XOR, AND, and OR gates. A **half-adder** can add two binary digits but lacks a carry function, while a **full-adder** incorporates a carry input, allowing for more complex addition in multi-bit numbers.

Boolean algebra simplifies circuit design by reducing the number of gates needed to perform a given function. Engineers use **Boolean identities**, such as the commutative, associative, and distributive laws, to manipulate logical expressions. For example, the identity A + AB = A allows an engineer to eliminate unnecessary terms in a circuit, saving resources and improving efficiency. These simplifications are critical in large-scale designs, where even small optimizations can significantly impact performance and cost.

Boolean algebra also introduces **De Morgan's Theorems**, which are particularly useful for circuit simplification. The theorems state that:

1.   ¬(A + B) = ¬A ¬B

2. $\neg(AB) = \neg A + \neg B$

These rules allow engineers to replace combinations of AND and OR gates with their opposites, often simplifying the design or making it more cost-effective to implement with available components.

Sequential circuits, unlike combinational ones, depend not only on current inputs but also on previous states. These circuits require memory elements, such as **flip-flops**, to store and recall binary data. Flip-flops are constructed using gates in specific configurations, enabling them to maintain their state until a triggering event changes it. For example, a **D flip-flop** captures the value of its input when a clock signal transitions, storing it for future use. This behavior is foundational for creating registers, counters, and other memory-based components.

Logic gates and Boolean algebra extend into the design of **finite state machines (FSMs)**, which model systems with defined states and transitions. FSMs are used in applications ranging from vending machines to network protocols. By leveraging Boolean logic, engineers define the conditions under which a system transitions between states, ensuring predictable and reliable operation.

Another important application is in the development of **programmable logic devices (PLDs)**, such as field-programmable gate arrays (FPGAs). These devices allow engineers to configure logic gates and Boolean functions dynamically, enabling rapid prototyping and customized circuit behavior. FPGAs rely heavily on Boolean algebra during design, as engineers program the device by defining logical relationships between inputs and outputs.

Logic gates are also central to **arithmetic logic units (ALUs)**, the part of a CPU responsible for performing mathematical and logical operations. ALUs combine a variety of logic circuits to execute tasks like addition, subtraction, bitwise operations, and comparisons. Boolean expressions define each operation, ensuring that the ALU processes data accurately and efficiently.

The integration of logic gates into **digital signal processing (DSP)** systems demonstrates their versatility. In DSP applications, gates are used to filter, modify, and analyze binary representations of analog signals. For example, logic gates can construct digital filters that remove noise from audio signals or sharpen video images.

Error detection and correction systems also rely heavily on Boolean algebra. Techniques like **parity generation** use XOR gates to calculate parity bits, which help identify errors in transmitted data. More sophisticated systems, like **Hamming codes**, use combinations of gates to both detect and correct errors, ensuring the integrity of data in communication and storage systems.

Another critical use of logic gates is in **control systems**, where Boolean logic dictates decision-making processes. For instance, industrial automation systems use programmable logic controllers (PLCs) with gate-based logic to monitor sensors and control machinery. These systems must operate in real time, making the simplicity and speed of logic gates invaluable.

As circuits grow in complexity, engineers use **circuit simulation software** to design and test logic gates virtually. Programs like SPICE or Verilog allow engineers to model gate behavior, verify Boolean expressions, and identify potential errors before committing to physical manufacturing. These tools streamline the design process and ensure that circuits meet performance specifications.

Even in emerging fields like **quantum computing**, Boolean principles inform foundational research. While quantum systems use qubits rather than binary bits, certain logic operations still mirror classical Boolean gates. For example, quantum equivalents of the NOT gate, like the Pauli-X gate, manipulate qubit states in ways analogous to classical logic.

The universality and simplicity of Boolean algebra and logic gates make them indispensable to computer engineering. Their ability to transform abstract logic into physical systems enables engineers to create everything from basic circuits to highly complex computing architectures. These foundational tools continue to evolve alongside technology, adapting to new challenges and applications.

Overview of Computer Architecture

Computer architecture refers to the conceptual design and fundamental operational structure of a computer system. It focuses on how hardware components interact to execute instructions and achieve computational tasks. This foundational field of computer engineering blends theoretical principles with practical design, enabling the efficient development of hardware systems that meet specific performance goals.

At the core of computer architecture is the **Central Processing Unit (CPU)**, often referred to as the brain of a computer. The CPU executes instructions, processes data, and manages the flow of information between hardware components. It is composed of three main parts: the **Arithmetic Logic Unit (ALU)**, the **Control Unit (CU)**, and **registers**. The ALU performs mathematical and logical operations, such as addition, subtraction, AND, and OR. The CU decodes instructions fetched from memory and directs other components to execute them. Registers serve as high-speed storage areas for data that the CPU is actively working on.

The **memory hierarchy** is another crucial aspect of computer architecture. Memory is divided into levels based on speed, cost, and capacity. At the top of the hierarchy is **cache memory**, a small and fast memory unit located close to or within the CPU. It stores frequently accessed data to reduce the time needed to fetch information from slower memory. Below the cache is **main memory** (RAM), which temporarily holds data and instructions for active processes. The lowest level, **secondary storage**, includes hard drives and SSDs, which provide long-term data storage but are much slower compared to cache and RAM.

Instruction handling in a CPU is governed by the **instruction set architecture (ISA)**, which defines the set of instructions a processor can execute. The ISA acts as a bridge between hardware and software, outlining how machine code is interpreted by the CPU. Common ISAs include x86, ARM, and RISC-V. Each instruction specifies an operation, such as loading data, performing arithmetic, or branching to another part of the program. The complexity of the ISA impacts the CPU's design, performance, and energy efficiency.

Modern CPUs leverage **pipelining** to enhance performance. Pipelining divides the execution of instructions into distinct stages, such as fetching, decoding, executing, and writing back results. By overlapping these stages, multiple instructions can be processed simultaneously. For instance, while one instruction is being executed, the next can be decoded, and another fetched. This parallelism increases the throughput of the processor, but careful management is required to handle dependencies and ensure correct results.

The concept of **parallel processing** extends beyond pipelining. Multi-core processors, which contain multiple independent CPUs (cores) on a single chip, allow for concurrent execution of tasks. This design significantly improves performance for applications that can be divided into smaller, independent workloads. Each core operates in parallel, sharing memory and resources with others, enabling faster processing of data-heavy tasks like video rendering or scientific simulations.

Another vital element of computer architecture is **input/output (I/O) systems**, which facilitate communication between the computer and external devices. I/O systems handle data transfer to and from peripherals such as keyboards, monitors, printers, and storage drives. The architecture of I/O systems ensures efficient and reliable data transfer, often relying on **buses**—shared communication pathways that connect components. For instance, the PCIe (Peripheral Component Interconnect Express) bus is widely used for high-speed communication between the CPU and devices like GPUs and SSDs.

Memory management is integral to computer architecture, ensuring the effective use of memory resources. The operating system (OS) handles tasks like allocating memory to programs, swapping data between RAM and disk storage, and managing virtual memory. **Virtual memory** allows a system to use more memory than physically available by temporarily storing data on disk and accessing it as needed. This abstraction simplifies programming and ensures that memory is utilized efficiently.

The design of **cache memory** is particularly critical to system performance. Cache operates on the principle of **locality**, which predicts that programs frequently reuse the same data (temporal locality) or data near previously accessed locations (spatial locality). By storing such data closer to the CPU, cache reduces latency and increases processing speed. Most modern processors implement multi-level caches (L1, L2, and L3), each with varying sizes and speeds to optimize data retrieval.

Branch prediction is another architectural feature aimed at improving CPU efficiency. During instruction execution, conditional branches (e.g., if-else statements) can disrupt the pipeline if the CPU waits to determine the branch outcome. To avoid delays, modern processors predict the most likely path the program will take and continue executing instructions along that path. If the prediction is correct, the pipeline proceeds without interruption. If it's wrong, the CPU discards the speculative instructions and corrects its course.

The **microarchitecture** of a processor defines how the ISA is implemented in hardware. It includes detailed design choices such as the number of execution units, the size of caches, and the layout of functional components. Two prominent design approaches are **CISC (Complex Instruction Set Computing)** and **RISC (Reduced Instruction Set Computing)**. CISC architectures, like x86, include a wide variety of complex instructions, enabling more functionality per instruction. In contrast, RISC architectures, such as ARM and RISC-V, use simpler instructions that can be executed more quickly, often requiring fewer hardware resources.

Computer architecture also encompasses **graphics processing units (GPUs)**, specialized processors designed for parallel workloads. Unlike CPUs, which excel at executing a few tasks sequentially, GPUs are optimized for executing thousands of smaller tasks simultaneously. This makes them ideal for applications like rendering graphics, training machine learning models, and running scientific simulations. GPU architecture prioritizes high-throughput parallelism, with hundreds or thousands of smaller cores designed to handle massive data sets efficiently.

Storage architecture has an important part in system performance and reliability. Traditional hard drives use spinning disks and magnetic read/write heads to store data, while **solid-state drives (SSDs)** rely on NAND flash memory for faster data access. Advances in storage technologies, such as NVMe (Non-Volatile Memory Express), have further reduced storage access latency, making it a critical component in modern high-performance systems. Emerging technologies like **persistent memory** aim to bridge the gap between volatile RAM and long-term storage, offering fast, byte-addressable storage that retains data when powered off.

In distributed computing environments, **network architecture** becomes a critical extension of computer architecture. Systems like data centers rely on interconnected servers to process and store vast amounts of data. High-speed network interfaces and protocols, such as InfiniBand and Ethernet, are essential for minimizing latency and maximizing throughput in these setups. Distributed systems also require careful management of memory coherence and resource sharing, especially in tightly coupled architectures like shared-memory multiprocessors.

Another key component of computer architecture is **power efficiency**, which has become increasingly important in the design of modern systems. Techniques like **dynamic voltage and frequency scaling (DVFS)** allow processors to adjust their power consumption based on workload demands, balancing performance and energy use. Power efficiency is particularly critical for mobile devices, where battery life is a primary concern, and for data centers, where energy costs are substantial.

The concept of **instruction-level parallelism (ILP)** is an advanced aspect of computer architecture that seeks to execute multiple instructions simultaneously within a single core. Superscalar architectures achieve ILP by using multiple execution units, allowing the CPU to dispatch and execute several instructions in parallel. This requires sophisticated scheduling and dependency management to ensure that operations are performed in the correct order.

The advent of **heterogeneous computing** has added another dimension to computer architecture. In heterogeneous systems, different types of processors—such as CPUs, GPUs, and specialized accelerators—work together to execute tasks. These systems take advantage of the strengths of each processor type, optimizing performance for specific workloads. For example, CPUs handle general-purpose tasks, while GPUs accelerate parallel computations, and dedicated AI accelerators, like Google's Tensor Processing Unit (TPU), are tailored for machine learning.

Finally, **emerging trends** in computer architecture point to exciting possibilities. **Quantum computing** introduces entirely new paradigms, leveraging quantum bits (qubits) instead of traditional binary bits. While still in its infancy, quantum computing has the potential to solve problems that are intractable for classical systems, such as large-scale optimization and cryptography. Similarly, **neuromorphic computing** aims to mimic the structure and functionality of biological neural networks, enabling highly efficient and adaptive processing for tasks like pattern recognition.

Computer architecture continues to evolve, driven by advances in technology and the growing demand for more powerful, efficient, and adaptable systems. Each development builds on established principles, pushing the boundaries of what computers can achieve. As we continue to integrate computing into every aspect of life, the design and optimization of computer architectures will remain at the forefront of innovation.

Introduction to Algorithms

An **algorithm** is a precise, step-by-step process for solving a specific problem or performing a task. In computer engineering, algorithms serve as the foundation for programming and system design. They define how data is processed, analyzed, and manipulated, ensuring tasks are completed efficiently and accurately. Algorithms exist at every level of computing, from basic arithmetic operations to complex machine learning models, making their understanding essential for anyone working in the field.

At their core, algorithms are defined by their **inputs, outputs, and process steps**. For an algorithm to be effective, it must be well-defined and unambiguous, with each step explicitly describing what action to take. Inputs are the data provided to the algorithm, and outputs are the results produced after processing. For example, in a sorting algorithm, the input might be an unsorted list of numbers, and the output would be the same list arranged in ascending or descending order.

Algorithms are typically evaluated based on two main criteria: **correctness** and **efficiency**. Correctness ensures that the algorithm produces the expected result for all valid inputs. Efficiency, on the other hand, measures how quickly and resourcefully an algorithm completes its task. In computer engineering, this often involves analyzing an algorithm's **time complexity** (how runtime scales with input size) and **space complexity** (how memory usage scales with input size).

Time complexity is expressed using **Big-O notation**, which provides an upper bound on an algorithm's growth rate. For instance, an algorithm with a complexity of $O(n)$ grows linearly with the size of the input, meaning the time required doubles as the input size doubles. In contrast, $O(n^2)$ represents a quadratic relationship, where the runtime increases quadratically with the input size. Understanding Big-O notation is crucial for evaluating and comparing algorithms, especially when dealing with large datasets.

One of the simplest and most well-known algorithms is **linear search**. In a linear search, the algorithm examines each element in a list one by one until it finds the target value or reaches the end of the list. While easy to implement, linear search has a time complexity of $O(n)$, making it inefficient for large datasets. A more optimized approach for sorted data is **binary search**, which repeatedly divides the search interval in half, reducing the time complexity to $O(\log n)$. Binary search demonstrates how leveraging data structure properties can significantly improve algorithm performance.

Sorting is another fundamental task in computing, and numerous algorithms exist to accomplish it. **Bubble sort**, one of the simplest sorting algorithms, repeatedly compares adjacent elements and swaps them if they are in the wrong order. While its simplicity makes it a common teaching tool, its time complexity of $O(n^2)$ makes it impractical for large datasets. More efficient algorithms, such as **merge sort** and **quick sort**, divide the input into smaller segments, sort them individually, and then combine the results. Merge sort guarantees a time complexity of O(n log n), while quick sort often achieves this on average but can degrade to $O(n^2)$ in the worst case.

Divide and conquer is a powerful paradigm demonstrated by merge sort and quick sort. In this approach, a problem is broken into smaller subproblems, solved independently, and then combined to form the solution. This methodology is particularly effective for complex problems, as dividing tasks into manageable pieces often reduces overall computational effort. Divide and conquer forms the basis of many algorithms, including those used for matrix multiplication and computational geometry.

Efficient data handling often requires algorithms for organizing and accessing information. **Hashing** is one such technique, widely used in tasks like database indexing, cryptography, and data retrieval. A **hash function** maps data elements (keys) to fixed-size values (hashes), enabling rapid lookups and insertions in structures like hash tables. For example, a well-designed hash table allows average-case operations like search, insert, and delete to run in O(1) time, making it highly efficient for large-scale applications.

Another important category is **graph algorithms**, used to model and solve problems involving networks. Graphs consist of vertices (nodes) connected by edges, representing relationships like social connections, roadmaps, or communication links. **Breadth-first search (BFS)** and **depth-first search (DFS)** are fundamental graph traversal algorithms. BFS explores nodes level by level, ensuring the shortest path is found in unweighted graphs, while DFS explores as far as possible along one branch before backtracking. These algorithms are crucial for applications such as finding routes, detecting cycles, and analyzing network structures.

Shortest-path algorithms, like **Dijkstra's algorithm** and the **Bellman-Ford algorithm**, find the minimum distance between nodes in weighted graphs. Dijkstra's algorithm uses a priority queue to select the next closest node, ensuring efficient computation for graphs with non-negative edge weights. Bellman-Ford, while slower, can handle graphs with negative weights, offering more flexibility. Another advanced approach, **Floyd-Warshall**, computes shortest paths between all pairs of nodes, albeit with higher time complexity.

In optimization problems, algorithms like **greedy algorithms** and **dynamic programming** are indispensable. Greedy algorithms make locally optimal choices at each step, hoping to arrive at a globally optimal solution. For example, the **Huffman coding algorithm**, used in data compression, builds a prefix-free binary tree by repeatedly combining the least frequent elements. Greedy methods are fast and simple but may fail to find the best solution for certain problems.

Dynamic programming addresses this limitation by breaking problems into overlapping subproblems and storing their solutions to avoid redundant computations. A classic example is the **Knapsack problem**, where the goal is to maximize the value of items that can fit into a limited-capacity bag. By solving subproblems and combining their results, dynamic programming achieves optimal solutions efficiently. Algorithms like **Fibonacci sequence generation** and **matrix chain multiplication** also benefit from this approach.

Algorithms also are critical in managing and processing large datasets. **Sorting and searching algorithms** are commonly used in databases and search engines. For instance, **heap sort** organizes data into a binary heap structure, ensuring efficient sorting in O(n log n) time. Search engines leverage algorithms like **PageRank**, which assigns importance scores to web pages based on their link structures, ensuring relevant results appear at the top.

In computational biology, algorithms are used to analyze DNA sequences, predict protein structures, and study genetic variations. Algorithms like **Smith-Waterman** and **Needleman-Wunsch** perform sequence alignment, identifying similarities between genetic data. These approaches use dynamic programming to find optimal matches, helping researchers understand evolutionary relationships and identify mutations.

The rise of artificial intelligence (AI) has further expanded the scope of algorithms. **Machine learning algorithms**, such as decision trees, neural networks, and support vector machines, analyze large datasets to make predictions or classify data. These algorithms rely on optimization techniques like **gradient descent**, which iteratively adjusts parameters to minimize error. Reinforcement learning, another subset of AI, uses algorithms like Q-learning to enable agents to learn through trial and error.

Algorithms also power cryptography, ensuring secure communication in an increasingly digital world. **Encryption algorithms**, like AES (Advanced Encryption Standard) and RSA (Rivest–Shamir–Adleman), protect data by transforming it into unreadable forms. RSA, for instance, uses modular arithmetic and prime factorization to encrypt and decrypt messages. Hashing algorithms, like SHA-256, are essential for digital signatures and blockchain technologies, where data integrity and security are paramount.

In addition to solving practical problems, algorithms are designed for specialized computational tasks. **Fourier transform algorithms**, like the Fast Fourier Transform (FFT), decompose signals into their frequency components, enabling applications in image processing, audio compression, and telecommunications. The **discrete cosine transform (DCT)**, a related algorithm, underpins compression standards like JPEG for digital images and MP3 for audio files.

Algorithms also underpin **real-time systems**, where tasks must be completed within strict deadlines. Scheduling algorithms determine the order in which processes are executed, ensuring timely performance in applications like robotics, aerospace systems, and medical devices. **Rate-monotonic scheduling** and **earliest deadline first** are common approaches used in real-time operating systems.

The advent of quantum computing has introduced new classes of algorithms that leverage quantum principles. **Shor's algorithm**, for instance, efficiently factors large integers, posing challenges for traditional encryption systems. **Grover's algorithm** provides a quadratic speedup for unsorted database searches. These quantum algorithms, while still in their infancy, have the potential to revolutionize fields like cryptography, optimization, and drug discovery.

As computer systems become more complex, algorithms continue to evolve, addressing new challenges and expanding their applications across diverse domains. Each algorithm, whether simple or sophisticated, is a carefully crafted solution to a specific computational problem, driving innovation in computer engineering and beyond.

Software vs. Hardware Engineering

Software engineering and **hardware engineering** are two interdependent pillars of computer engineering. Both disciplines aim to design and develop functional systems, but their focus and methods are fundamentally different. Software engineering is concerned with creating instructions that tell hardware what to do, while hardware engineering focuses on building the physical machines capable of executing those instructions. Understanding the distinctions and synergies between these fields is critical for anyone entering computer engineering.

At its core, hardware engineering deals with the **physical components** of a computer system. This includes designing circuits, processors, memory modules, and interfaces for input and output devices. Hardware engineers use principles from electrical engineering and physics to create machines that perform computations accurately and reliably. They work on designing chips, developing printed circuit boards (PCBs), and testing the durability and efficiency of physical systems. Modern hardware engineers often leverage tools like CAD (computer-aided design) software to simulate and validate their designs before manufacturing.

In contrast, software engineering involves writing, testing, and maintaining **code**—the instructions that enable hardware to perform tasks. Software engineers use programming languages like C++, Python, or Java to develop applications, operating systems, and embedded programs. Their focus is on algorithms, user experience, and ensuring the software functions correctly under various conditions. Debugging, version control, and software testing are integral parts of this process, ensuring that programs run smoothly and efficiently.

One key difference between the two disciplines is the **level of abstraction** they operate at. Hardware engineering works with physical components that must adhere to the laws of physics, while software engineering operates in a virtual realm constrained only by logic and computational rules. For instance, a hardware engineer might design a processor with a specific clock speed and number of cores, while a software engineer develops code to optimize how those cores are utilized.

Timing and concurrency highlight the intricate relationship between software and hardware. Hardware engineers design processors with features like pipelining and parallel execution to maximize throughput. Software engineers, in turn, must write programs that leverage these features without causing bottlenecks. Multithreading, for example, allows software to execute multiple tasks simultaneously, but it requires careful management to avoid race conditions and deadlocks.

The role of **memory management** differs significantly between the two fields. Hardware engineers design memory hierarchies, from cache to RAM to storage, optimizing for speed and efficiency. They determine how data flows between these levels and how access times are minimized. Software engineers, however, write programs that interact with this memory architecture, ensuring efficient allocation and deallocation of resources. They use concepts like pointers, memory pools, and garbage collection to manage memory effectively in their code.

Embedded systems are a prime example of the close collaboration required between software and hardware engineers. These systems consist of hardware specifically designed for a dedicated task, combined with software that controls it. Examples include automotive control systems, medical devices, and consumer electronics. Hardware engineers create specialized processors or controllers for these applications, while software engineers write the firmware that governs their behavior. Any misalignment between the two can lead to system failures, making tight integration essential.

While hardware engineering involves substantial upfront costs, such as manufacturing specialized chips or testing physical prototypes, software engineering has its challenges in terms of **scalability and maintainability**. Writing clean, modular, and extensible code ensures that software can evolve over time, accommodating new hardware or user requirements. Software engineers must also address compatibility issues, ensuring programs work across different hardware configurations.

Debugging techniques further illustrate the contrast between the two fields. Hardware engineers often rely on oscilloscopes, logic analyzers, and simulators to test circuits and identify issues. They examine electrical signals, voltages, and timing diagrams to ensure hardware behaves as expected. Software engineers, on the other hand, use tools like debuggers, profilers, and static code analyzers to identify logic errors, memory leaks, or performance bottlenecks in their programs.

The **development lifecycle** also varies significantly. Hardware engineering follows a linear, sequential process. Once hardware is manufactured, changes are costly and time-consuming, making thorough testing and validation critical before production. Software development, however, often follows iterative methodologies like Agile or DevOps. Code can be updated, patched, or rewritten even after deployment, providing greater flexibility but also requiring continuous testing and version control.

The rapid advancement of **hardware capabilities** continuously shapes the work of software engineers. For instance, the rise of multi-core processors and GPUs has driven software engineers to write parallel and optimized code to take full advantage of these architectures. Similarly, developments in hardware accelerators like TPUs (Tensor Processing Units) for machine learning require new software frameworks and algorithms that align with their capabilities.

Power efficiency is another domain where the relationship between software and hardware is evident. Hardware engineers design components to minimize power consumption, particularly in portable devices like smartphones and laptops. They incorporate features like dynamic voltage scaling or sleep modes into hardware. Software engineers complement this by writing energy-efficient code, ensuring applications utilize resources judiciously and do not drain battery life unnecessarily.

The rise of **cloud computing** has further blurred the lines between software and hardware engineering. Hardware engineers design the servers, networking equipment, and storage devices that power data centers. Meanwhile, software engineers create the virtualization layers, orchestration tools, and applications that run on this hardware. The collaboration between the two ensures that cloud infrastructure can handle massive workloads reliably and cost-effectively.

Security is another shared responsibility. Hardware engineers develop features like encryption modules, secure boot mechanisms, and trusted execution environments to protect systems at the hardware level. Software engineers build on these capabilities, writing secure code that resists attacks like buffer overflows or SQL injection. Together, they create layered defenses that protect systems against increasingly sophisticated threats.

Despite their differences, the two fields often converge in the design of **application-specific integrated circuits (ASICs)** and **field-programmable gate arrays (FPGAs)**. ASICs are custom chips tailored for specific tasks, such as cryptocurrency mining or AI inference. FPGAs, on the other hand, allow engineers to reprogram hardware logic after manufacturing. These technologies require hardware engineers to design efficient circuits and software engineers to write the programs that configure and operate them.

The evolution of **edge computing** illustrates the growing synergy between software and hardware engineering. Edge devices, such as IoT sensors or smart cameras, process data locally rather than relying on centralized cloud servers. Hardware engineers design these devices to balance performance, power efficiency, and cost, while software engineers write lightweight, optimized code that runs within the device's resource constraints. This collaboration enables real-time processing and decision-making in applications like autonomous vehicles or industrial automation.

As hardware becomes more sophisticated, the role of **abstraction layers** in software becomes increasingly important. Abstraction layers, such as operating systems or APIs, simplify the complexities of interacting with hardware. For example, an OS abstracts the details of memory allocation, input/output operations, and device drivers, enabling software developers to focus on higher-level functionality without worrying about low-level hardware specifics.

The growing adoption of **artificial intelligence (AI)** and machine learning has introduced unique challenges for both fields. Hardware engineers design accelerators like GPUs or neural processing units (NPUs) to handle the intense computational demands of AI workloads. Software engineers develop frameworks like TensorFlow or PyTorch, enabling developers to train and deploy AI models efficiently. This combination of specialized hardware and optimized software has made AI applications like voice recognition and autonomous navigation possible.

The advent of **quantum computing** represents an entirely new frontier for software and hardware engineers. Quantum hardware engineers design qubits and quantum gates that operate under entirely different principles than classical bits. Software engineers, in turn, create quantum algorithms and programming languages, like Qiskit, to harness the potential of these machines. The collaboration between these disciplines is critical for realizing the promise of quantum computing.

In modern computer engineering, the boundaries between software and hardware engineering are increasingly blurred. Many engineers work at the intersection of the two fields, developing systems where hardware and software are co-designed for optimal performance. This trend reflects the growing complexity and interconnectedness of computing systems, where innovation often arises from the seamless integration of physical and virtual components.

CHAPTER 2: COMPUTER ARCHITECTURE

Components of a Computer System

A computer system consists of several interconnected components, each performing specific tasks to process, store, and transfer data. These components work together to execute instructions, solve problems, and manage resources efficiently. Understanding the function and design of each part provides a clear picture of how computers operate at their core.

The **Central Processing Unit (CPU)** is the heart of any computer system. It performs arithmetic, logical, and control operations by interpreting instructions stored in memory. The CPU consists of three primary components: the **Arithmetic Logic Unit (ALU)**, the **Control Unit (CU)**, and **registers**. The ALU handles mathematical calculations and logical comparisons, while the CU fetches and decodes instructions, orchestrating the flow of data across the system. Registers are small, high-speed storage areas within the CPU, temporarily holding data and instructions during processing. Modern CPUs are designed with features like pipelining and multiple cores to increase efficiency and handle parallel tasks.

Memory is another critical component. **Primary memory**, commonly referred to as **Random Access Memory (RAM)**, stores data and instructions that the CPU actively uses. RAM is volatile, meaning its contents are lost when the computer is powered off. This high-speed storage allows the CPU to quickly retrieve the information it needs for processing. The size and speed of RAM directly impact a computer's performance, particularly for tasks requiring significant data manipulation, such as video editing or large-scale simulations.

In addition to RAM, the **cache memory** serves as a faster, smaller storage located closer to the CPU. Cache stores frequently accessed data, reducing the time the CPU spends retrieving information from slower memory levels. Cache is organized in multiple levels — L1, L2, and sometimes L3 — each progressively larger and slower. L1 cache is the smallest but fastest, integrated directly into the CPU core. Efficient use of cache dramatically improves processing speeds, especially for repetitive tasks.

Secondary storage provides non-volatile, long-term storage for data and software. Devices like hard disk drives (HDDs) and solid-state drives (SSDs) fall into this category. HDDs use magnetic platters to store data, making them cost-effective for large capacities, but slower compared to SSDs. SSDs, on the other hand, use flash memory, offering much faster access times and greater durability since they lack moving parts.

Secondary storage also includes removable media like USB drives, DVDs, and memory cards, which facilitate data transfer and backup.

The **motherboard** connects all these components, acting as the main circuit board of the system. It houses the CPU, memory modules, and expansion slots for additional hardware, such as graphics cards or network adapters. The motherboard also provides pathways, or **buses**, for data to travel between components. These buses vary in speed and function, with some dedicated to high-speed data transfer (e.g., PCIe) and others for general communication (e.g., USB or SATA).

Input devices allow users to interact with the computer by providing data and commands. Keyboards, mice, and touchscreens are common examples, each converting user actions into signals the computer can process. More specialized input devices include scanners, game controllers, and microphones, which cater to specific applications. The quality and responsiveness of these devices often impact the overall user experience.

Conversely, **output devices** communicate results back to the user. Monitors display visual information, speakers produce sound, and printers create physical copies of digital documents. Modern monitors, such as LED or OLED displays, offer high resolutions and refresh rates, enhancing clarity and responsiveness. Output devices must be compatible with the system's hardware and software to function seamlessly.

Storage controllers manage the interaction between the CPU and storage devices. These controllers oversee data flow, error detection, and device communication protocols like SATA for HDDs or NVMe for SSDs. They optimize performance by ensuring that data is transferred efficiently, often using techniques like buffering or prefetching to reduce latency.

The **graphics processing unit (GPU)** is a specialized processor designed to handle visual computations. Originally created for rendering images and videos, GPUs now power a variety of applications, including gaming, machine learning, and scientific simulations. Unlike CPUs, which excel at sequential processing, GPUs are built for parallel workloads, using thousands of smaller cores to process data simultaneously. Discrete GPUs, installed as separate hardware units, provide greater power and flexibility compared to integrated GPUs, which are built into the CPU.

Power supplies convert electrical energy into the appropriate voltage and current levels required by the system. A **power supply unit (PSU)** ensures that all components receive stable and reliable power, protecting them from surges and fluctuations. PSUs are rated by their wattage capacity and efficiency, with higher-quality models providing cleaner and more efficient power delivery. A poorly designed PSU can lead to system instability or even hardware failure.

The **network interface card (NIC)** enables communication between a computer and other devices over a network. NICs, either integrated into the motherboard or installed as expansion cards, manage data transfer protocols, such as Ethernet or Wi-Fi. Advanced NICs also support offloading tasks like packet filtering, reducing the load on the CPU and improving network performance.

Cooling systems are essential for maintaining the reliability of computer components. CPUs, GPUs, and other high-performance parts generate significant heat during operation. Without adequate cooling, these components can overheat, leading to reduced performance or permanent damage. Cooling solutions include air cooling, which uses fans to dissipate heat, and liquid cooling, which circulates coolant through heat exchangers for more efficient thermal management. High-end systems may employ both methods for optimal temperature control.

Peripheral devices, such as printers, external storage, or webcams, extend the functionality of a computer system. While not essential for core operations, these devices add convenience and enable specific tasks. Peripheral connections are facilitated by **I/O ports** like USB, HDMI, or Thunderbolt, which provide high-speed communication between the computer and external hardware.

BIOS (Basic Input/Output System) or its modern counterpart, **UEFI (Unified Extensible Firmware Interface)**, initializes hardware during the boot process and provides a basic interface between the operating system and the system firmware. Stored in non-volatile memory on the motherboard, the BIOS/UEFI performs a power-on self-test (POST) to check the functionality of components before loading the operating system. This ensures that hardware is ready for use and correctly configured.

Modern systems also rely on **virtualization technologies**, which allow a single physical machine to host multiple virtual machines (VMs). Virtualization is managed by software called hypervisors, which allocate CPU, memory, and storage resources to each VM. Hardware support for virtualization, such as Intel VT-x or AMD-V, enhances performance by enabling direct interaction between VMs and the physical hardware.

The **chipset**, often integrated into the motherboard, acts as a communication hub for the system. It connects the CPU to memory, storage, and peripheral devices, managing data flow and resource allocation. Modern chipsets are divided into two main sections: the **northbridge**, responsible for high-speed communication (e.g., between CPU and RAM), and the **southbridge**, which handles lower-speed devices like USB ports and SATA controllers.

Sound cards process audio signals, converting digital data into analog sound waves for speakers or headphones. While many motherboards include integrated audio, dedicated sound cards provide superior sound quality and advanced features, such as surround sound or noise reduction. These cards are essential for professional audio production or immersive gaming experiences.

Lastly, **expansion cards** allow users to add functionality to their computer systems. Common examples include network cards, RAID controllers, and additional GPUs. Expansion cards use slots like PCIe to connect to the motherboard, ensuring high-speed communication and integration with the rest of the system.

Understanding the components of a computer system is fundamental to designing, building, and optimizing hardware for various applications. Each part contributes to the system's overall functionality, reliability, and performance.

Instruction Set Architectures (ISA)

An **Instruction Set Architecture (ISA)** defines the interface between software and hardware. It is a fundamental part of computer architecture that specifies the set of instructions a processor can execute, how these instructions are encoded, and how they interact with memory, registers, and other hardware components. The ISA serves as a bridge, enabling programmers and compilers to write software that hardware can interpret and execute.

ISAs are categorized by the number and type of instructions they support. Two primary types are **CISC (Complex Instruction Set Computing)** and **RISC (Reduced Instruction Set Computing)**. CISC architectures, such as x86, include a broad and diverse set of instructions, some of which perform complex tasks in a single operation. This design minimizes the number of instructions required to execute a program but often requires more hardware complexity and slower execution for individual instructions. In contrast, RISC architectures, such as ARM and RISC-V, feature a smaller, simpler instruction set. These instructions are highly optimized for speed and often execute in a single clock cycle, enabling greater performance and efficiency in modern processors.

The **instruction formats** within an ISA define how instructions are encoded into binary, specifying fields such as the operation code (opcode), source and destination registers, and immediate values. Some ISAs use fixed-length instruction formats, simplifying decoding and execution, while others employ variable-length formats, offering flexibility at the cost of complexity. For example, x86 uses variable-length instructions, while ARM uses fixed-length instructions for efficiency in embedded systems and mobile devices.

A critical aspect of ISAs is how they handle **registers** and **memory addressing**. Registers are small, high-speed storage locations within the CPU, and their size and count vary across ISAs. For instance, ARM processors commonly feature 16 general-purpose registers, while x86 processors include a smaller set with specialized purposes. Addressing modes, such as immediate, direct, indirect, and indexed, define how an instruction accesses data in memory. Advanced ISAs support multiple addressing modes to accommodate diverse programming requirements.

Modern ISAs include extensions to support specific workloads. For example, Intel's x86 architecture incorporates **SSE (Streaming SIMD Extensions)** and **AVX (Advanced Vector Extensions)** for high-performance vector processing, essential in tasks like scientific simulations and multimedia processing. ARM's ISA includes **NEON**, a similar extension for mobile and embedded applications. These enhancements improve performance by enabling parallelism within a single instruction.

Instruction-level parallelism (ILP) is another area influenced by ISAs. Techniques like **pipelining**, **superscalar execution**, and **out-of-order execution** rely on ISA design to maximize CPU utilization. RISC architectures, with their simpler instructions, often achieve higher levels of ILP, making them well-suited for applications requiring efficient parallel processing.

Some ISAs are designed for specific domains. **VLIW (Very Long Instruction Word)** architectures, such as Intel's Itanium, bundle multiple instructions into a single, wide word, allowing hardware to execute them simultaneously. While VLIW achieves high parallelism, it places greater complexity on the compiler, which must identify and schedule independent instructions.

Open ISAs like **RISC-V** are gaining popularity in academia and industry due to their flexibility and extensibility. RISC-V allows engineers to customize the instruction set for specific applications, such as IoT devices or specialized accelerators. This open approach contrasts with proprietary ISAs like x86 or ARM, which are controlled by specific companies and require licensing fees.

An ISA's design influences many aspects of computer architecture, including memory management, interrupt handling, and power efficiency. It defines how instructions interact with the **cache hierarchy**, whether through direct mappings or advanced features like prefetching. Additionally, ISA compatibility ensures software portability across generations of hardware. For example, software written for an older x86 processor can run on newer models due to backward compatibility, a critical feature for enterprise and legacy systems.

System Performance Metrics

Evaluating the performance of a computer system involves analyzing various **metrics** that quantify its efficiency, speed, and resource utilization. These metrics are essential for understanding how well a system handles tasks and identifying areas for improvement. In computer architecture, performance is measured at multiple levels, from individual components like CPUs and memory to the overall system.

One of the most basic and widely used metrics is **clock speed**, measured in gigahertz (GHz). Clock speed represents the number of cycles a processor executes per second. While higher clock speeds often indicate faster performance, they don't always guarantee it. The efficiency of instruction execution, the presence of parallelism, and bottlenecks in memory or I/O can significantly impact overall performance, even with high clock speeds.

Instructions per cycle (IPC) is another critical metric that measures how many instructions a processor can execute in a single clock cycle. IPC depends on the processor's design, including its pipelining, branch prediction, and out-of-order execution capabilities. A processor with a higher IPC can perform more work at the same clock speed, demonstrating the importance of architectural optimizations beyond raw frequency.

Throughput measures the amount of work a system can complete over a given period, often expressed as tasks or instructions per second. This metric is particularly relevant for multi-core and parallel systems, where overall performance depends on the effective utilization of multiple processing units. **Latency**, on the other hand, refers to the time it takes to complete a single task or instruction. High throughput does not always imply low latency, as tasks may be queued or executed in parallel.

Memory latency and bandwidth are key factors in system performance. Latency is the time it takes to retrieve data from memory, while bandwidth measures the volume of data that can be transferred in a given time. Modern systems implement features like multi-level caches and prefetching to reduce latency and increase effective bandwidth. For example, a large L3 cache reduces the frequency of slow main memory accesses, significantly improving performance in data-intensive applications.

In addition to memory, **I/O performance** is important in overall system efficiency. Metrics like **input/output operations per second (IOPS)** and **data transfer rate** quantify the performance of storage devices and peripherals. SSDs typically offer higher IOPS compared to HDDs, making them better suited for tasks requiring rapid data access, such as database transactions or video editing.

Power efficiency is becoming increasingly important as systems grow in complexity and energy costs rise. Metrics like **performance per watt** evaluate how effectively a system converts electrical power into useful computation. Architects achieve power efficiency through techniques like dynamic voltage scaling, low-power states, and optimized circuit design. This metric is especially critical in mobile devices, where battery life is a major constraint, and in data centers, where energy efficiency directly affects operational costs.

Cache hit rate is a specific metric used to assess the efficiency of the memory hierarchy. A high hit rate indicates that most memory requests are satisfied by the cache, reducing the need for slower main memory accesses. Conversely, a low hit rate may signal poor cache design or suboptimal memory access patterns in software.

Another important metric is **execution time**, often considered the ultimate measure of system performance. Execution time includes not only processing delays but also stalls caused by memory latency, branch mispredictions, or contention for shared resources. Architects aim to minimize execution time through optimizations at every level, from microarchitecture to software design.

Speedup is a relative metric used to compare the performance of different systems or configurations. For example, speedup can quantify the benefit of adding more cores to a processor or upgrading from an HDD to an SSD. Speedup is often expressed as a ratio: Speedup = Execution time (baseline) / Execution time (improved). Achieving linear speedup—where performance increases proportionally with resources—is challenging due to bottlenecks and overheads.

Scalability measures how well a system maintains performance as workloads increase or hardware resources are added. A scalable system can efficiently utilize additional cores, memory, or storage without significant performance degradation. Scalability is particularly important in cloud computing and distributed systems, where workloads can vary widely.

Utilization is another key metric, indicating how effectively a system uses its available resources. For example, CPU utilization measures the percentage of time the processor is actively executing instructions versus idling. Low utilization may signal underpowered workloads or inefficiencies, while high utilization can lead to overheating and throttling.

Benchmarks provide standardized methods for evaluating system performance. These benchmarks simulate real-world workloads, such as rendering images, running databases, or compiling software, offering a consistent basis for comparison. Examples include SPEC (Standard Performance Evaluation Corporation) benchmarks for CPUs and 3DMark for GPUs. Architects use benchmark results to validate designs and identify performance bottlenecks.

Network performance metrics, such as latency, throughput, and packet loss, are critical for distributed systems and cloud environments. Latency affects real-time applications like video conferencing, while throughput determines the system's ability to handle large data transfers. Packet loss can degrade performance, requiring retransmissions and reducing efficiency.

Performance metrics guide architectural decisions and optimizations, ensuring systems meet the demands of modern computing tasks.

Parallel Processing and Multithreading

Parallel processing and **multithreading** are two fundamental concepts in modern computer architecture that enable systems to execute multiple tasks simultaneously, improving performance and efficiency. These techniques exploit the inherent parallelism in many computational problems, reducing execution time and optimizing resource utilization. Understanding how parallel processing and multithreading work requires a deep dive into the architecture of processors and the mechanisms that support concurrency.

Parallel processing involves dividing a task into smaller subtasks and executing them simultaneously across multiple processing units. This is achieved through **multi-core processors**, which integrate multiple independent cores onto a single chip. Each core operates as a separate processor, capable of executing its own instructions and accessing memory. By distributing tasks among these cores, parallel processing increases throughput, especially for applications with computationally intensive workloads like scientific simulations, machine learning, and video rendering.

The effectiveness of parallel processing depends on the degree of parallelism in the workload. Tasks are categorized as **embarrassingly parallel** or **tightly coupled**, depending on their independence. Embarrassingly parallel tasks, such as image processing or Monte Carlo simulations, can be divided into smaller units with minimal dependency, making them ideal for parallel execution. Tightly coupled tasks, like fluid dynamics simulations, require frequent communication and synchronization between processing units, adding complexity to the parallelization process.

In multi-core systems, **shared memory** is a common architecture for facilitating parallel processing. All cores share access to a single memory space, simplifying data sharing but introducing challenges like contention and consistency. To mitigate these issues, processors implement **cache coherence protocols**, such as MESI (Modified, Exclusive, Shared, Invalid), to ensure that changes made to cached data by one core are visible to others. These protocols maintain data consistency but can add latency due to frequent communication between caches.

Another approach to parallelism is **distributed memory**, where each processing unit has its own local memory. Distributed memory systems are common in clusters and supercomputers, where nodes communicate through high-speed interconnects like InfiniBand or Ethernet. This architecture eliminates contention but requires explicit data sharing through message-passing protocols like **MPI (Message Passing Interface)**, adding complexity to software design.

Parallel processing also extends to specialized hardware like **GPUs (Graphics Processing Units)**, which are optimized for massively parallel workloads. Unlike CPUs, GPUs feature thousands of smaller cores designed for simultaneous execution of simple tasks, making them well-suited for applications like deep learning and molecular modeling. GPU programming models, such as CUDA and OpenCL, allow developers to write code that exploits this hardware parallelism, leveraging architectures with hierarchical memory structures and warp scheduling.

Instruction-level parallelism (ILP) complements task-level parallelism by enabling the simultaneous execution of multiple instructions within a single core. Techniques like **pipelining, superscalar execution**, and **out-of-order execution** improve ILP by overlapping instruction fetch, decode, and execute stages. Superscalar processors can issue multiple instructions per cycle, while out-of-order execution reorders instructions to maximize resource utilization and avoid stalls caused by data dependencies.

Multithreading takes parallel processing to a finer level of granularity by dividing a single task into multiple threads of execution. Threads are lightweight processes that share the same memory space but execute independently, enabling concurrent execution within a single core or across multiple cores. **Hardware multithreading** implements this at the architectural level, allowing a core to switch between threads when one is stalled, such as during a memory access.

Simultaneous multithreading (SMT), commonly known as hyper-threading in Intel processors, takes this concept further by enabling a single core to execute multiple threads in parallel. SMT leverages idle execution units within the core, increasing utilization and throughput. For example, while one thread performs arithmetic operations, another can execute memory loads, maximizing the use of available hardware resources.

The efficiency of multithreading depends on workload characteristics and software design. Applications with a high degree of **thread-level parallelism (TLP)**, such as web servers or database management systems, benefit significantly from multithreading. However, poorly designed multithreaded programs can suffer from issues like **race conditions**, where multiple threads access shared resources simultaneously, leading to unpredictable behavior. Proper synchronization mechanisms, such as locks, semaphores, and atomic operations, are essential to ensure correctness.

In multi-core and multithreaded environments, the operating system is critical in **scheduling**. The scheduler allocates CPU time to threads, balancing load across cores and minimizing context-switching overhead. Advanced scheduling algorithms, such as **priority scheduling** and **work-stealing**, optimize resource utilization by assigning tasks dynamically based on system load and task priority.

Parallel processing and multithreading also impact **memory hierarchies**. Shared data structures in multithreaded programs can lead to **false sharing**, where threads on different cores modify adjacent memory locations in the same cache line. This causes unnecessary invalidation and reloads, degrading performance. Optimizing memory access patterns and aligning data structures to cache boundaries can mitigate these issues, improving throughput in parallel systems.

To facilitate parallel programming, various frameworks and libraries provide abstractions for developers. **OpenMP**, for example, simplifies the creation of parallel loops and tasks in C, C++, and Fortran by using compiler directives. **Threading Building Blocks (TBB)**, developed by Intel, offers a higher-level approach to parallelism, focusing on task-based rather than thread-based programming. These tools abstract away many low-level details, allowing developers to focus on parallelizing their algorithms effectively.

While parallel processing and multithreading offer significant performance gains, they are not without challenges. **Amdahl's Law** provides a theoretical limit on the speedup achievable through parallelism. According to this law, the speedup is constrained by the portion of the task that must be executed serially. For example, if 90% of a task can be parallelized, the maximum speedup achievable is 10x, regardless of how many processors are added. This highlights the importance of minimizing serial components in software to fully exploit parallel architectures.

Gustafson's Law offers a more optimistic perspective, emphasizing that as problem size increases, the parallelizable portion of the workload often grows, enabling greater speedup. This principle is particularly relevant in fields like scientific computing, where larger datasets and more complex simulations naturally benefit from parallel processing.

Power efficiency is another critical consideration in parallel processing. While adding more cores and threads increases performance, it also raises power consumption and heat generation. Modern processors address this through techniques like **dynamic voltage and frequency scaling (DVFS)** and **asymmetric multiprocessing (AMP)**, where cores with different power-performance profiles are used for specific tasks. For instance, ARM's **big.LITTLE architecture** pairs high-performance cores with energy-efficient ones, dynamically switching between them based on workload demands.

Parallelism is not limited to CPUs and GPUs; it extends to specialized accelerators like **TPUs (Tensor Processing Units)** and **FPGAs (Field-Programmable Gate Arrays)**. TPUs, designed for machine learning workloads, execute matrix operations in parallel with high efficiency. FPGAs, on the other hand, allow developers to configure hardware logic to perform specific tasks concurrently, offering flexibility and performance gains for applications like real-time analytics and cryptography.

Parallel processing also underpins **cloud computing** and **distributed systems**, where tasks are divided across multiple machines. Technologies like **MapReduce** and **Apache**

Spark enable large-scale data processing by distributing computations across clusters of servers. These frameworks handle parallelism at the software level, abstracting complexities like fault tolerance and data distribution from developers.

Real-time systems, such as those used in aerospace or automotive applications, rely on parallel processing and multithreading to meet strict timing constraints. These systems often include **real-time operating systems (RTOS)**, which prioritize tasks based on deadlines and ensure deterministic execution. Parallelism in such environments is carefully managed to prevent latency and guarantee predictable behavior.

The growing importance of **heterogeneous computing** has added new dimensions to parallel processing and multithreading. Heterogeneous systems combine CPUs, GPUs, and other accelerators, each optimized for specific workloads. Parallel programming models like **CUDA, OpenCL**, and **SYCL** enable developers to distribute tasks across these diverse architectures, maximizing performance and energy efficiency.

Parallel processing and multithreading have become essential for addressing the demands of modern computing. Whether through multi-core processors, GPUs, or distributed systems, these techniques enable the efficient execution of complex tasks, driving advancements in fields ranging from artificial intelligence to scientific research. As hardware evolves, the principles of parallelism and concurrency will remain central to the design and optimization of computer systems.

CHAPTER 3: DIGITAL LOGIC AND CIRCUIT DESIGN

Combinational Logic Circuits

Combinational logic circuits are a cornerstone of digital design, used to create systems where outputs depend only on the current inputs. Unlike sequential circuits, they have no memory or feedback loops. Each output is a direct result of a logical combination of input values, making these circuits predictable and efficient for many applications. They form the building blocks for larger digital systems, including arithmetic units, encoders, decoders, and multiplexers.

At the heart of every combinational logic circuit are **logic gates** — AND, OR, NOT, NAND, NOR, XOR, and XNOR. These gates manipulate binary signals, where each signal represents one of two states: 0 (low) or 1 (high). Each gate performs a specific Boolean operation, and by combining gates in various ways, you can build circuits that execute complex logical functions. For example, an AND gate outputs 1 only if all its inputs are 1, while an OR gate outputs 1 if at least one input is 1. These simple behaviors are foundational for more advanced designs.

Truth tables describe how combinational circuits behave. For a given set of inputs, a truth table lists all possible input combinations and their corresponding outputs. Consider a simple circuit with two inputs (A and B) and an OR gate. The truth table for this circuit would include four rows, representing all combinations of A and B (00, 01, 10, 11). The corresponding outputs would show 0, 1, 1, and 1, respectively, based on the OR gate's operation. Truth tables provide a clear, systematic way to define a circuit's behavior.

Designing combinational circuits often starts with a **Boolean expression**. For example, suppose you need a circuit where the output is 1 if either input A is 1, or both inputs B and C are 1. The Boolean expression for this would be: Output = $A + (B \cdot C)$. This expression is then translated into a circuit diagram using the appropriate gates. Simplifying Boolean expressions using laws of Boolean algebra, such as De Morgan's Theorems, helps minimize the number of gates needed, reducing costs and improving performance.

Minimization techniques are essential in combinational circuit design. Reducing the number of gates or connections not only saves physical space in hardware but also lowers power consumption and enhances reliability. Tools like Karnaugh maps (K-maps) help designers visually simplify Boolean expressions. A K-map organizes truth table outputs into a grid, allowing patterns to emerge that indicate redundant terms or opportunities for simplification. For more complex designs, software tools like logic synthesizers automate this process.

One of the simplest and most common combinational circuits is the **half-adder**, which performs the addition of two binary digits. It has two inputs (A and B) and two outputs: sum and carry. The sum output is calculated using an XOR gate, while the carry output uses an AND gate. For example, if A = 1 and B = 1, the sum output is 0 (since 1 XOR 1 = 0), and the carry output is 1 (since 1 AND 1 = 1). The half-adder is a foundational circuit used in arithmetic operations.

Building on the half-adder, the **full-adder** extends this functionality by adding a third input, the carry-in, to handle multi-bit binary addition. A full-adder outputs a sum and a carry-out. By chaining multiple full-adders together, you can construct **ripple carry adders**, capable of adding binary numbers of arbitrary length. For instance, a 4-bit ripple carry adder uses four full-adders, each passing its carry-out to the next stage.

Other combinational circuits include **multiplexers (MUX)**, which select one of many input signals to pass to the output based on control signals. A 2-to-1 multiplexer has two inputs, one control signal, and one output. When the control signal is 0, the first input is selected; when it's 1, the second input is selected. Multiplexers are invaluable in applications requiring data selection or routing, such as in CPUs or communication systems.

Demultiplexers (DEMUX) perform the reverse operation of multiplexers, taking a single input and directing it to one of several outputs based on control signals. A 1-to-4 demultiplexer, for example, has one input, two control signals, and four outputs. Only one output is active at a time, corresponding to the value of the control signals. Demultiplexers are commonly used in memory addressing and data distribution.

Encoders and **decoders** are additional types of combinational circuits. An encoder converts multiple active input signals into a smaller number of outputs. For example, a 4-to-2 binary encoder takes four input lines and outputs a 2-bit binary code representing the active input. Decoders perform the opposite function, converting binary-coded inputs into a one-hot output representation. A 2-to-4 decoder takes a 2-bit binary input and activates one of four output lines based on the input value. These circuits are widely used in communication systems, data compression, and hardware control.

For error detection and correction, combinational circuits like **parity generators** and **checkers** are used. A parity generator produces a parity bit that ensures the total number of 1s in a data word is even or odd, depending on the chosen parity scheme. Parity checkers validate the integrity of received data by comparing the parity bit with the data word. If they don't match, an error is detected. Such circuits are fundamental in error-correcting codes and digital communication.

Another essential circuit is the **comparator**, which determines the relationship between two binary numbers. A comparator outputs signals indicating whether one number is greater than, less than, or equal to the other. For example, an 8-bit comparator would compare two 8-bit binary inputs and produce three outputs: one for each possible relationship. Comparators are frequently used in sorting algorithms, control systems, and signal processing.

In practical applications, combinational circuits are often designed using **hierarchical approaches**. Instead of building large circuits from scratch, designers use pre-designed modules, such as adders or multiplexers, to create complex systems. This modular approach simplifies design, testing, and debugging while ensuring scalability. For instance, in a CPU, the arithmetic logic unit (ALU) is built using combinational circuits like adders, subtractors, and logical operators.

Timing is a critical factor in combinational circuit design. Although outputs depend solely on inputs, the propagation delay through gates affects the time it takes for the output to stabilize. Propagation delay is the time required for a signal to travel through a gate, and it accumulates as the signal passes through multiple gates in a circuit. Minimizing propagation delay is crucial for high-speed systems, and this often involves balancing the number of gates and optimizing their placement.

Hardware description languages (HDLs), such as **VHDL** and **Verilog**, are used to design and simulate combinational circuits. These languages allow engineers to describe circuits at a high level, specifying logical behavior rather than physical layout. Once the design is verified through simulation, it can be synthesized into hardware using tools like field-programmable gate arrays (FPGAs) or application-specific integrated circuits (ASICs). This process streamlines the transition from design to implementation.

Sequential Logic Circuits

Sequential logic circuits are a foundational aspect of digital logic and circuit design. Unlike combinational circuits, the outputs of sequential circuits depend not only on the current inputs but also on the circuit's past states. This dependence on previous states is achieved through the inclusion of memory elements, allowing these circuits to store information. Sequential circuits are essential for building complex systems like registers, counters, and finite state machines.

The basic building blocks of sequential logic are **flip-flops** and **latches**, which are memory elements capable of storing a single bit of data. A latch is a level-sensitive device, meaning its output changes as long as the control signal (often called the enable signal) is active. In contrast, a flip-flop is edge-triggered, changing its state only at a specific transition (rising or falling edge) of a clock signal. This distinction makes flip-flops more suitable for synchronous designs, where all components operate in lockstep with a central clock.

The **SR (Set-Reset) latch** is the simplest form of a latch. It consists of two cross-coupled NOR gates (or NAND gates) that hold their state until an input signal changes it. The set input drives the latch to store a logic 1, while the reset input drives it to store a logic 0. However, the SR latch has a limitation: when both set and reset inputs are active simultaneously, it produces an undefined state. This issue is addressed in other memory elements like the **D (Data) latch**, which ensures only one input (data) determines the stored value while the enable signal controls when the value is updated.

Flip-flops build on the functionality of latches, adding synchronization with a clock signal. The **D flip-flop**, derived from the D latch, updates its output only on the clock's edge. This behavior ensures that changes to the input do not propagate to the output until the clock triggers the update, providing precise timing control in sequential systems. The **JK flip-flop** improves on the SR latch by eliminating its undefined state. With two inputs (J and K), it can toggle its state, set it to 1, or reset it to 0 based on the input combination. The **T (Toggle) flip-flop**, a simplification of the JK flip-flop, toggles its state on every clock pulse when its input is active.

Sequential circuits are categorized as either **synchronous** or **asynchronous**. In synchronous circuits, all state changes are coordinated by a global clock signal. This approach ensures predictability and simplifies design but may introduce delays due to the time required for the clock signal to propagate through the system. Asynchronous circuits, on the other hand, do not rely on a global clock. Instead, they use local signals or events to trigger state changes, offering faster response times but increasing design complexity and susceptibility to timing issues like **race conditions**.

One of the most common applications of sequential logic is the **counter**, which generates a sequence of binary numbers. A simple binary counter consists of a series of flip-flops connected in a ripple configuration, where the output of one flip-flop drives the clock input of the next. Each clock pulse increments the counter by one. This type of counter is called a **ripple counter** because changes propagate sequentially through the flip-flops, introducing delays. To address this, **synchronous counters** use a single clock signal to drive all flip-flops simultaneously, eliminating the ripple effect and enabling faster operation.

Shift registers are another vital application of sequential circuits. A shift register consists of a chain of flip-flops connected in series, with the output of one feeding the input of the next. These circuits move data bits in a specific direction (left or right) with each clock pulse. Shift registers are used in data serialization, where parallel data is converted into a serial stream for transmission, and vice versa. For example, in communication systems, data bits can be shifted out one at a time to match the serial transmission protocol.

Sequential circuits also underpin the design of **finite state machines (FSMs)**, which are used to model and control systems with distinct states and transitions. FSMs are composed of memory elements to store the current state and combinational logic to determine the next state and outputs. FSMs are widely used in embedded systems, control units, and protocol design. For example, a vending machine can be modeled as an FSM, with states representing actions like waiting for input, validating coins, dispensing items, and returning change.

The interaction between **combinational logic** and **memory elements** is critical in sequential circuit design. The memory stores the current state, while the combinational logic calculates the next state based on inputs and the current state. This feedback loop creates a system that evolves over time, enabling dynamic behavior. Proper timing and synchronization are essential to avoid errors, such as **glitches**, where transient changes in combinational logic outputs cause incorrect state transitions.

Clock skew is a critical consideration in synchronous sequential circuits. Clock skew occurs when the clock signal arrives at different parts of the circuit at slightly different times due to variations in wiring length or delays in the clock distribution network. If not addressed, skew can lead to timing violations, causing the circuit to behave unpredictably. Designers mitigate skew by carefully balancing clock paths or using clock distribution techniques like buffers and phase-locked loops (PLLs).

In sequential circuits, the concept of **setup and hold times** defines the timing constraints for flip-flops. The setup time is the minimum duration before the clock edge during which the input must remain stable, while the hold time is the minimum duration after the clock edge during which the input must not change. Violating these constraints can result in **metastability**, where the flip-flop output oscillates or becomes unpredictable. Metastability is particularly problematic in systems with asynchronous inputs, requiring techniques like synchronization or metastability-hardened designs to mitigate its effects.

Advanced sequential circuits often include **counters with additional functionality**, such as up/down counters that increment or decrement based on control signals. Other variations, like ring counters and Johnson counters, use feedback connections to generate specific sequences. For example, a 4-bit ring counter cycles through four states, with only one flip-flop active at any given time, while a Johnson counter cycles through twice as many states using the same number of flip-flops.

Designing efficient sequential circuits requires a deep understanding of **timing diagrams**, which illustrate the relationship between inputs, outputs, and the clock signal over time. Timing diagrams help engineers visualize and verify the behavior of sequential circuits, ensuring that state transitions occur as expected. For example, a timing diagram for a shift register shows how data moves through each flip-flop with successive clock pulses.

Sequential logic circuits are also integral to **state encoding**, the process of assigning binary codes to the states of an FSM. State encoding affects the complexity of the circuit, as some encodings lead to simpler combinational logic for state transitions. Common encoding methods include **binary encoding**, where states are represented with the minimum number of bits, and **one-hot encoding**, where each state is represented by a single active bit. One-hot encoding simplifies the logic at the cost of increased hardware usage.

In asynchronous sequential circuits, the lack of a clock signal introduces additional challenges. Designers must carefully analyze and resolve **hazards**, which are unintended changes in circuit output caused by variations in signal propagation times. **Static hazards** occur when an output briefly changes when it should remain constant, while **dynamic hazards** involve unintended oscillations. Mitigating these hazards often requires adding redundant gates or modifying the circuit's design to stabilize transitions.

Sequential logic circuits are also at the core of **timers and delay circuits**, which introduce controlled delays into digital systems. For example, a digital timer can use a series of flip-flops to count clock pulses, generating an output signal after a specific interval. These circuits are widely used in applications ranging from clock generation to event sequencing.

Design tools like **Verilog** and **VHDL** simplify the creation and simulation of sequential circuits. These hardware description languages allow designers to specify the behavior of flip-flops, counters, and FSMs at a high level, abstracting away low-level implementation details. Simulation tools then verify the design's functionality before it is synthesized into hardware.

Sequential circuits, with their ability to store and manipulate states over time, form the backbone of digital systems. They enable dynamic, state-dependent behavior, making them indispensable in applications ranging from simple timers to complex control systems.

Finite State Machines

Finite state machines (FSMs) are a fundamental concept in digital logic and circuit design. They are mathematical models used to describe systems that transition between a finite number of states based on input signals. FSMs are particularly useful for designing control systems, communication protocols, and sequential circuits, where system behavior depends on past events and current inputs.

FSMs consist of three main components: **states**, **transitions**, and **outputs**. States represent specific conditions or configurations of the system, transitions define how the system moves from one state to another based on inputs, and outputs are the signals or actions produced by the machine in a given state. For example, in a traffic light controller, states might represent the lights (red, yellow, or green), transitions are triggered by timers or sensors, and outputs control the lights' illumination.

There are two primary types of FSMs: **Moore machines** and **Mealy machines**. In a Moore machine, outputs depend solely on the current state. This makes Moore machines simpler to analyze and debug, as outputs are stable regardless of input fluctuations. In contrast, a Mealy machine's outputs depend on both the current state and the inputs. This allows for faster response times, as outputs can change immediately in response to input changes without waiting for a state transition. The choice between Moore and Mealy machines depends on the specific requirements of the application.

The design process for an FSM begins with **state identification**. Engineers define all possible states the system can occupy and describe the conditions that trigger transitions between these states. For instance, in a vending machine, states might include waiting for input, verifying payment, dispensing the item, and returning change. Each state corresponds to a distinct part of the system's behavior.

After defining the states, a **state transition diagram** is created. This graphical representation shows states as circles and transitions as directed arrows between them, labeled with the input conditions that trigger each transition. State diagrams provide a clear overview of system behavior, making it easier to identify errors or missing transitions during the design phase.

The next step involves assigning binary codes to each state. This process, known as **state encoding**, determines how states are represented in the circuit. Common encoding methods include **binary encoding**, which uses the minimum number of bits, and **one-hot encoding**, where each state is represented by a single active bit. Binary encoding minimizes hardware usage, while one-hot encoding simplifies the combinational logic required for state transitions.

FSMs are implemented using a combination of **sequential and combinational logic**. Flip-flops or latches store the current state, while combinational logic calculates the next state and outputs based on the current state and inputs. Timing is managed by a clock signal, ensuring that state transitions occur synchronously. This structure creates a reliable and predictable system.

One practical application of FSMs is in **communication protocols**, such as those used in network devices. For example, an FSM can model the behavior of a UART (Universal Asynchronous Receiver-Transmitter), handling tasks like detecting start bits, shifting data into registers, and generating parity bits. Each state corresponds to a step in the protocol, and transitions occur based on input signals from the communication line.

FSMs are also used in **embedded systems** for controlling devices like washing machines, elevators, and robotics. In these applications, the FSM acts as a decision-making unit, guiding the system through predefined sequences of operations. For instance, in a washing machine, states might include filling, washing, rinsing, and spinning, with transitions triggered by timers or sensor inputs.

When designing FSMs, engineers must carefully consider **timing and synchronization**. In synchronous FSMs, a clock signal ensures that state transitions occur simultaneously across the circuit. However, in asynchronous FSMs, where transitions are triggered by input events rather than a clock, timing issues like **races** and **hazards** can arise. These must be addressed through careful design and simulation.

Simulation tools like **ModelSim** or **Quartus Prime** are often used to verify FSM designs before implementation. These tools allow engineers to test state transitions, inputs, and outputs under various conditions, ensuring that the system behaves as expected. Once verified, the design can be synthesized into hardware using tools like FPGAs or ASICs.

FSMs are versatile and widely used in digital design. They provide a structured approach to modeling complex systems, enabling engineers to create reliable and efficient circuits for a broad range of applications.

Designing Simple Digital Systems

Designing simple digital systems involves combining logic gates, flip-flops, and other basic components to perform a specific function. The process begins with a clear understanding of the system's requirements, including the inputs, outputs, and desired behavior. Engineers translate these requirements into a logical framework, which can then be implemented using digital circuits.

The first step in designing a digital system is defining the **functional specification**. This includes listing all inputs and outputs, describing how the system should respond to each input, and specifying timing requirements if applicable. For instance, in a digital clock, inputs might include a reset signal and a clock pulse, while outputs display hours, minutes, and seconds.

Next, engineers create a **truth table** or functional description of the system. A truth table systematically lists all possible input combinations and their corresponding outputs. For example, if the system is a binary adder, the truth table includes all possible combinations of input bits and their summed outputs. This step ensures that all edge cases and scenarios are accounted for in the design.

Once the behavior is defined, the system is expressed using **Boolean algebra**. Boolean expressions describe the logical relationships between inputs and outputs. For example, in a simple voting system where the output is 1 if at least two of three inputs are 1, the

Boolean expression is Y = AB + AC + BC. This expression forms the basis for the circuit design.

Minimizing Boolean expressions is an essential step to reduce hardware complexity. Tools like **Karnaugh maps** (K-maps) help identify redundant terms and simplify expressions visually. For larger systems, software tools like logic synthesizers perform this task automatically, optimizing the design for efficiency and cost.

The simplified Boolean expression is then translated into a **logic circuit diagram**, showing the arrangement of gates, flip-flops, and other components. The diagram serves as a blueprint for the physical implementation of the system. Engineers ensure that the circuit is modular, breaking it into smaller, reusable subsystems to simplify testing and debugging.

For sequential systems, designers incorporate **timing elements** like flip-flops and clocks. These elements ensure that outputs are updated synchronously, avoiding errors caused by timing mismatches. For example, in a shift register, each flip-flop is triggered by the same clock signal, moving data one step at a time with each pulse.

Simulation is an integral part of digital system design. Engineers use tools like **Verilog** or **VHDL** to describe the system's behavior and simulate its operation under different conditions. These simulations verify that the design meets functional specifications and timing requirements before committing to hardware.

Digital systems are often implemented using **field-programmable gate arrays (FPGAs)** or **application-specific integrated circuits (ASICs)**. FPGAs offer flexibility, allowing designers to test and modify the system after deployment, while ASICs provide a permanent, cost-effective solution for mass production. The choice depends on the application's requirements, budget, and expected lifecycle.

For simple systems, **modular design** is crucial. Modular designs break the system into smaller blocks, each performing a specific function. For instance, in a calculator, one module might handle addition, another multiplication, and a third display management. This approach simplifies testing, as each module can be verified independently before integration.

Digital systems must also account for **error detection and correction**. Techniques like parity checking and cyclic redundancy checks (CRCs) ensure data integrity, especially in communication or storage applications. Including these mechanisms adds reliability to the system, preventing issues caused by hardware faults or external interference.

In applications requiring interaction with external devices, designers incorporate **I/O interfaces**. These interfaces, such as USB or SPI, enable the system to communicate with sensors, actuators, or other peripherals. Properly designing these interfaces ensures compatibility and minimizes latency.

Designing simple digital systems is both a creative and methodical process. Following a structured approach — from specification to implementation — engineers create systems that perform reliably, efficiently, and effectively.

CHAPTER 4: MICROPROCESSORS AND EMBEDDED SYSTEMS

Anatomy of a Microprocessor

A **microprocessor** is the brain of a computer system. It processes data, executes instructions, and manages the flow of information between other components. At its core, the microprocessor is a highly integrated circuit that contains millions, often billions, of transistors. These transistors work together to perform operations like arithmetic, logic, control, and data movement at incredible speeds.

The central component of a microprocessor is the **Arithmetic Logic Unit (ALU)**. This part performs mathematical operations such as addition, subtraction, multiplication, and division. It also handles logical operations like AND, OR, XOR, and NOT. The ALU is designed to process binary data, and it interacts directly with other parts of the processor to execute instructions. For example, when a program instructs the microprocessor to add two numbers, the ALU performs this operation and sends the result to another unit for further processing or storage.

The **Control Unit (CU)** is another essential part of the microprocessor. It acts as a conductor, directing the flow of data and instructions throughout the processor. The control unit fetches instructions from memory, decodes them to understand what needs to be done, and then signals other parts of the processor to perform the required operations. This sequence of actions — fetch, decode, execute — is called the **instruction cycle**, and the CU ensures that every step is completed in the correct order.

Registers are small, high-speed memory locations inside the microprocessor. They temporarily store data that the processor is actively working on, such as intermediate results, instruction addresses, or control information. Registers come in different types, each serving a specific purpose. General-purpose registers hold operands for the ALU, while special-purpose registers, like the Program Counter (PC), track the address of the next instruction to be executed. Another important register, the Instruction Register (IR), holds the instruction currently being processed.

The **clock** is a critical component that sets the tempo for the processor's operations. The clock generates a continuous series of electrical pulses, and the microprocessor uses these pulses to synchronize its actions. The speed of the clock, measured in gigahertz (GHz), determines how many cycles the processor can complete in one second. For instance, a 3 GHz processor performs three billion cycles per second. However, raw clock speed is only part of the performance equation. Other architectural factors, such as pipelining and parallelism, also are important.

Modern microprocessors include **pipelines**, which divide the instruction cycle into discrete stages such as fetch, decode, execute, and write-back. By overlapping these stages, the processor can work on multiple instructions simultaneously, significantly increasing throughput. For example, while one instruction is being executed, the next can be decoded, and another can be fetched from memory. This design maximizes the utilization of the processor's resources, but it requires careful handling of dependencies between instructions to avoid stalls.

Cache memory is another integral part of the microprocessor. It stores frequently accessed data and instructions, reducing the time the processor spends retrieving information from slower main memory. Cache is typically organized into levels—L1, L2, and L3. L1 cache is the smallest and fastest, located directly on the processor core. L2 cache is slightly larger but slower, and L3 cache is shared among multiple cores in multi-core processors. Efficient cache management is critical for minimizing latency and boosting overall performance.

The **bus interface unit** connects the microprocessor to the rest of the system, facilitating communication with memory, input/output devices, and other peripherals. Data, instructions, and control signals travel along buses, which are shared communication pathways. Modern processors use advanced bus architectures, such as QuickPath Interconnect (QPI) or HyperTransport, to achieve high data transfer rates. The bus interface unit coordinates these transfers, ensuring that data flows smoothly between the microprocessor and external components.

Another critical feature of modern microprocessors is **branch prediction**. During program execution, the processor often encounters conditional instructions, such as "if-then" statements. To maintain efficiency, the processor predicts which branch of the condition will be taken and speculatively executes instructions along that path. If the prediction is correct, the processor saves time. If it's wrong, the processor discards the speculative results and executes the correct instructions. Advanced branch prediction algorithms minimize the performance impact of incorrect predictions, ensuring that pipelines remain full.

The **floating-point unit (FPU)** is a specialized component of the microprocessor designed to handle operations involving real numbers, such as scientific calculations or graphics processing. The FPU performs tasks like floating-point addition, multiplication, and division with high precision. While earlier microprocessors relied on external co-processors for floating-point operations, modern designs integrate the FPU directly into the chip for better performance and efficiency.

In multi-core processors, each core functions as an independent microprocessor, capable of executing its own instructions. Multi-core architectures enable **parallel processing**, where multiple cores work simultaneously on different tasks or threads. This design is particularly advantageous for applications like video editing, gaming, and scientific simulations, which can leverage multiple cores to process data in parallel. Shared resources, such as L3 cache and the memory bus, facilitate communication between cores, but they also introduce challenges like contention and coherence.

The **instruction set architecture (ISA)** defines the set of instructions the microprocessor can execute. Common ISAs include x86, ARM, and RISC-V, each optimized for different applications. The microprocessor's design is tightly coupled to its ISA, as it determines how instructions are fetched, decoded, and executed. For instance, x86 processors support a wide range of complex instructions, while ARM processors use a reduced instruction set optimized for power efficiency, making them ideal for mobile and embedded systems.

Power efficiency is a critical consideration in microprocessor design, especially for mobile devices and laptops. Features like **dynamic voltage and frequency scaling (DVFS)** allow the processor to adjust its power consumption based on workload demands. For example, when running lightweight applications, the processor reduces its clock speed and voltage to save energy. Conversely, during high-performance tasks, it operates at maximum capacity to deliver the required speed.

Microprocessors also include **security features** to protect against vulnerabilities like buffer overflows or unauthorized access. Technologies like Intel's **Trusted Execution Technology (TXT)** or AMD's **Secure Encrypted Virtualization (SEV)** provide hardware-level security by isolating sensitive data and ensuring that only trusted code executes in protected regions. These features are essential for safeguarding personal data, especially in cloud computing and enterprise environments.

The integration of **hardware accelerators** in modern microprocessors addresses specialized workloads like artificial intelligence, cryptography, and graphics processing. For instance, processors may include tensor processing units (TPUs) for machine learning or dedicated encryption engines for secure communication. These accelerators offload tasks from the main cores, enhancing performance and reducing energy consumption.

Hyper-threading and **simultaneous multithreading (SMT)** are techniques used to improve resource utilization in microprocessors. By allowing a single core to execute multiple threads simultaneously, these technologies increase throughput and enable better handling of multi-threaded applications. For example, while one thread waits for a memory operation to complete, another thread can use idle execution units, maximizing the processor's efficiency.

The **memory management unit (MMU)** handles the translation between virtual and physical memory addresses, enabling features like virtual memory and memory protection. The MMU uses a structure called a page table to map virtual addresses to physical locations in memory. This abstraction simplifies programming and allows multiple processes to share the same physical memory space without interference.

The **pipeline depth** of a microprocessor influences its performance and power consumption. Deeper pipelines allow for higher clock speeds by breaking instructions into smaller, more manageable stages. However, this also increases the penalty for mispredicted branches or pipeline stalls, as more instructions must be flushed and re-executed. Designers must balance pipeline depth with overall efficiency and workload characteristics.

Modern microprocessors are marvels of engineering, packing extraordinary complexity into a tiny package. Each component—from the ALU to the memory management unit—contributes to the processor's ability to execute billions of instructions per second with remarkable precision. By understanding the anatomy of a microprocessor, you gain insight into the intricate mechanisms that power modern computing systems.

Microcontroller vs. Microprocessor

Microcontrollers and **microprocessors** are central to modern computing and embedded systems, but their purposes and architectures differ significantly. Both are integrated circuits designed to process data, yet their target applications and internal components set them apart.

A **microprocessor** is the central unit in general-purpose computing systems, such as desktops, laptops, and servers. It focuses exclusively on data processing and computation, relying on external components like memory, input/output interfaces, and peripherals to function. In contrast, a **microcontroller** is a complete system on a chip (SoC). It integrates a processor, memory, and peripherals into a single package, making it ideal for embedded applications like home automation, automotive systems, and consumer electronics.

The primary distinction lies in their **integration levels**. A microprocessor handles complex computations and high-speed processing but requires external components like RAM, ROM, and timers to operate. For instance, an Intel Core i5 processor needs a motherboard, memory modules, and external I/O controllers to create a functional system. A microcontroller, such as an ARM Cortex-M3, comes with built-in RAM, ROM (or flash memory), timers, and communication interfaces like UART and SPI, providing a compact solution for specific tasks.

The **focus of applications** further differentiates them. Microprocessors are designed for performance and versatility, supporting multitasking, high-resolution graphics, and complex algorithms. They are the backbone of operating systems, large-scale simulations, and resource-intensive applications. Microcontrollers, on the other hand, are tailored for efficiency and simplicity in real-time, single-purpose systems. A microcontroller embedded in a washing machine, for example, controls the motor, monitors water levels, and manages user inputs, all within a constrained environment.

Cost is another significant factor. Microprocessors are generally more expensive due to their advanced capabilities, larger die sizes, and higher power requirements. In contrast, microcontrollers are cost-effective, making them suitable for mass-produced embedded systems. A typical 8-bit microcontroller, like the PIC16F877A, costs just a few dollars, while high-end microprocessors can run into hundreds of dollars.

Power consumption varies dramatically between the two. Microcontrollers are built for low-power environments and often include energy-saving modes, such as sleep or idle states, to minimize consumption. This makes them ideal for battery-powered devices like remote controls and IoT sensors. Microprocessors, with their higher clock speeds and demand for external components, consume significantly more power. For example, a typical microprocessor may require active cooling to dissipate heat, while a microcontroller often operates passively without additional cooling mechanisms.

Architecture is critical in their differences. Microcontrollers commonly use **Harvard architecture**, where separate memory buses handle program instructions and data. This allows simultaneous access to both, increasing speed and efficiency in control applications. Microprocessors typically use **von Neumann architecture**, where instructions and data share the same memory bus. While this simplifies design and supports complex operations, it introduces bottlenecks in memory access, especially under heavy workloads.

Microcontrollers generally operate at **lower clock speeds**, often in the range of 1 MHz to a few hundred MHz, which is sufficient for their intended tasks. Microprocessors, in contrast, run at speeds measured in GHz, allowing them to handle intensive operations like video rendering and machine learning. For instance, an ARM Cortex-M4 microcontroller might operate at 100 MHz, while an Intel Core i7 microprocessor could reach 3.5 GHz or higher.

The **instruction set architecture (ISA)** further distinguishes the two. Microcontrollers often use **RISC (Reduced Instruction Set Computing)** architectures, emphasizing simplicity and efficiency. RISC architectures, such as ARM's Cortex-M series, allow faster execution by using fewer, simpler instructions. Microprocessors frequently employ **CISC (Complex Instruction Set Computing)** architectures, like x86, which support a broad range of complex instructions optimized for general-purpose computing. The choice of ISA reflects the priorities of each device: efficiency for microcontrollers and versatility for microprocessors.

Microcontrollers excel in **real-time systems**, where precise timing and immediate responses are critical. Built-in timers, pulse-width modulation (PWM) units, and interrupt controllers enable microcontrollers to handle time-sensitive tasks effectively. For example, a microcontroller in an automotive system can react instantly to changes in sensor data, such as adjusting the throttle or deploying airbags. Microprocessors, while powerful, are not optimized for strict real-time constraints without additional hardware support.

Development tools for each also differ. Microcontrollers are often programmed using lightweight integrated development environments (IDEs) like MPLAB or Keil, with code written in C or assembly. These tools include features for debugging, simulation, and in-circuit programming. Microprocessor development typically involves more robust environments, such as Eclipse or Visual Studio, often working with complex operating systems like Linux or Windows. The learning curve for microprocessor development is steeper due to the system's complexity.

Communication capabilities are integral to both microcontrollers and microprocessors but implemented differently. Microcontrollers often include integrated peripherals for serial communication, such as UART, I2C, or SPI, making them ideal for interacting with sensors, actuators, and other embedded components. Microprocessors rely on external controllers for these functions, using more advanced communication protocols like PCIe, SATA, or Ethernet to connect with peripherals and other systems.

The choice between a microcontroller and a microprocessor often depends on the **scalability and flexibility** required for the application. For instance, a smart thermostat uses a microcontroller for its focused task of temperature control and communication with a central hub. In contrast, a gaming console, which needs to run complex software, manage high-resolution graphics, and support multiple peripherals, requires a microprocessor.

Microcontrollers also shine in **IoT (Internet of Things)** applications. Their low power consumption, integrated wireless modules, and compact size make them perfect for smart devices like fitness trackers, smart locks, and environmental sensors. Microprocessors, though less common in IoT endpoints, are essential in IoT gateways and servers, where processing and aggregation of data from multiple sensors occur.

Debugging and testing present unique challenges for each. Microcontrollers often include features like in-circuit debugging (ICD) or joint test action group (JTAG) interfaces, allowing developers to step through code and analyze hardware behavior in real-time. Microprocessor systems, with their complex interactions between hardware and software, require advanced debugging tools and techniques, such as emulators and virtualization platforms, to identify and resolve issues.

As technology evolves, the line between microcontrollers and microprocessors continues to blur. Modern microcontrollers incorporate advanced features like floating-point units (FPUs), DSP capabilities, and even AI accelerators, narrowing the gap in functionality. Meanwhile, microprocessors integrate more power-saving features and simplified designs, addressing some of their traditional limitations for embedded applications.

Despite these advancements, the fundamental differences in **design philosophy** remain. Microcontrollers prioritize integration, simplicity, and efficiency, catering to cost-sensitive, single-purpose applications. Microprocessors, with their modularity and computational power, excel in scenarios requiring high performance and flexibility. Understanding these distinctions allows engineers to make informed choices, ensuring that the selected device aligns with the specific requirements of their project.

Basics of Embedded Systems

Embedded systems are specialized computer systems designed to perform dedicated tasks within larger devices or applications. Unlike general-purpose computers, embedded systems are optimized for specific functions, often operating with constrained resources and strict performance requirements. They are found in everyday objects like home appliances, medical devices, automobiles, and industrial machinery.

The core of an embedded system is typically a **microcontroller** or a **microprocessor**. A microcontroller is a compact system-on-a-chip (SoC) that integrates a processor, memory, and peripherals in a single package. It is ideal for embedded applications that require cost-effectiveness and simplicity. A microprocessor, while more powerful, relies on external components like memory and I/O controllers, making it suitable for more complex systems. The choice between the two depends on the application's computational and integration requirements.

Embedded systems use **firmware**, a type of software stored in non-volatile memory, such as ROM or flash memory. Firmware provides the instructions the system needs to function, from initializing hardware at startup to executing specific control tasks. Unlike software in general-purpose computers, firmware is tightly coupled with the hardware and rarely changes, ensuring stability and reliability in operation.

Real-time operation is a key characteristic of many embedded systems. Real-time systems must respond to inputs or events within a predefined time frame, often measured in microseconds or milliseconds. For instance, in an automotive airbag system, the embedded system must detect a collision and deploy the airbag almost instantaneously to prevent injury. Missing this deadline would render the system ineffective, highlighting the importance of deterministic behavior in real-time embedded systems.

Embedded systems are typically designed to be **resource-efficient**, operating with limited processing power, memory, and energy. Low power consumption is especially critical in battery-powered devices like wearables or IoT sensors. Engineers achieve this efficiency by optimizing hardware design, selecting lightweight microcontrollers, and writing minimalistic, tightly integrated code.

Communication interfaces are vital in embedded systems, enabling interaction with other devices or subsystems. Common interfaces include UART, SPI, I2C, and CAN, each tailored for specific applications. For example, UART is widely used for serial communication, while CAN is preferred in automotive systems for its robustness and ability to handle multiple devices on a shared bus.

Sensors and actuators often serve as the input and output components of embedded systems. Sensors, such as temperature sensors or accelerometers, provide real-world data that the system processes to make decisions. Actuators, such as motors or relays, carry out physical actions based on the system's outputs. For instance, a home thermostat's embedded system reads temperature data from a sensor and adjusts the HVAC system through actuators to maintain the desired temperature.

The development of embedded systems involves **hardware-software co-design**, where hardware and software components are developed concurrently to meet the system's functional and performance requirements. This approach ensures seamless integration and optimizes resource usage. Engineers use tools like circuit simulators and hardware description languages (HDLs) to design hardware, while IDEs like Keil or MPLAB support software development.

Embedded systems often require **real-time operating systems (RTOS)** to manage tasks and ensure deterministic behavior. An RTOS provides scheduling, task prioritization, and resource management, enabling the system to handle multiple tasks simultaneously without missing deadlines. For example, an RTOS in a robotic arm ensures that motor control, sensor data processing, and user commands are executed in the correct order and within specific time constraints.

Security is another critical aspect of embedded systems, especially as devices become interconnected through IoT. Embedded systems must protect sensitive data and prevent unauthorized access. Engineers implement encryption, secure boot mechanisms, and authentication protocols to safeguard systems against threats like data breaches or malware attacks. For instance, a smart home system encrypts communication between devices to prevent attackers from intercepting or altering data.

The **design lifecycle** of an embedded system includes requirement analysis, hardware selection, software development, testing, and deployment. Engineers start by defining the system's functional requirements, such as input/output behavior, timing constraints, and environmental conditions. Based on these requirements, they select hardware components that meet performance and cost goals. Software development follows, with emphasis on efficient coding and thorough testing to ensure reliability.

Simulation and prototyping are essential steps in embedded system design. Simulation tools allow engineers to model system behavior before physical hardware is available, saving time and resources. Prototypes, often built using development boards like Arduino or Raspberry Pi, provide a testbed for validating hardware and software integration in real-world conditions.

Embedded systems have **limited user interfaces** compared to general-purpose computers. Many systems rely on simple indicators like LEDs, buttons, or small displays for interaction. More advanced systems, like car infotainment units, incorporate touchscreens and voice recognition for user-friendly operation. The interface design must balance functionality with simplicity, ensuring usability without overwhelming the system's resources.

Role of Real-Time Operating Systems (RTOS)

A **real-time operating system (RTOS)** is a specialized operating system designed to manage the execution of tasks in real-time systems, ensuring that critical operations are completed within strict deadlines. RTOS is indispensable in embedded systems where deterministic behavior is required, such as medical devices, industrial automation, and automotive safety systems.

An RTOS uses **scheduling algorithms** to prioritize and manage tasks efficiently. Unlike general-purpose operating systems, which focus on maximizing throughput, an RTOS ensures that high-priority tasks are executed on time, even under heavy workloads. Two common scheduling techniques are **preemptive scheduling** and **cooperative scheduling**. In preemptive scheduling, the RTOS interrupts lower-priority tasks to execute higher-priority ones, ensuring responsiveness. Cooperative scheduling relies on tasks voluntarily yielding control, making it simpler but less suited for systems with strict timing constraints.

The concept of **task prioritization** is central to an RTOS. Tasks are assigned priorities based on their importance and timing requirements. For example, in a pacemaker, monitoring the heart's electrical signals would have the highest priority, while logging data for later analysis might be a lower-priority task. The RTOS enforces these priorities, preventing low-priority tasks from delaying critical operations.

RTOS manages **real-time clocks and timers**, which are essential for scheduling and time-sensitive operations. Timers trigger events like periodic task execution or timeout detection, enabling the system to maintain precise timing. For instance, an RTOS in an autonomous vehicle uses timers to process sensor data at regular intervals, ensuring smooth navigation.

Task synchronization and communication are handled through **inter-task communication mechanisms**, such as message queues, semaphores, and mutexes. These tools enable tasks to share data and coordinate their actions without conflicts. For example, in a robotic arm, a sensor task might send position data to a control task through a message queue, ensuring that movements are accurately synchronized.

RTOS ensures efficient **resource management**, allocating CPU time, memory, and I/O resources among tasks. This is critical in embedded systems with limited resources, where inefficient usage can lead to performance bottlenecks or system crashes. Memory protection mechanisms in RTOS prevent tasks from accessing unauthorized memory regions, enhancing system stability and security.

RTOS supports **interrupt handling**, a feature that allows the system to respond quickly to external events. Interrupts temporarily pause the execution of a task to handle time-critical inputs, such as a button press or sensor signal. For example, an RTOS in an industrial machine prioritizes emergency stop signals through interrupts, ensuring immediate action.

The lightweight nature of RTOS makes it suitable for **embedded systems with constrained resources**. Unlike general-purpose operating systems, which require significant memory and processing power, an RTOS has a small footprint, enabling it to run efficiently on microcontrollers with limited RAM and CPU capabilities. For instance, FreeRTOS, a popular open-source RTOS, can run on systems with as little as a few kilobytes of memory.

RTOS is critical in **real-time communication protocols**, such as CAN, I2C, and SPI. It ensures that data is transmitted and processed within defined time frames, preventing delays or data loss. For example, in an automotive network, the RTOS manages communication between sensors, controllers, and actuators, maintaining the synchronization required for smooth operation.

Testing and debugging are streamlined in RTOS-based systems. Many RTOS implementations include tools for monitoring task execution, resource usage, and timing behavior. These tools help developers identify and resolve issues like priority inversions, where a high-priority task is delayed by lower-priority ones. Features like trace analysis provide detailed insights into system performance, enabling fine-tuning for optimal operation.

An RTOS is not a one-size-fits-all solution. Choosing the right RTOS depends on factors like task complexity, timing requirements, and hardware constraints. Options range from commercial RTOS solutions, such as VxWorks or QNX, to open-source alternatives like FreeRTOS or Zephyr. Each RTOS offers unique features, such as scalability, security, or compatibility with specific microcontrollers.

RTOS transforms embedded systems by providing structure, reliability, and deterministic performance. It enables the creation of responsive, efficient, and secure systems, meeting the demanding requirements of modern real-time applications.

CHAPTER 5: MEMORY SYSTEMS AND STORAGE

Memory Hierarchies: Cache, RAM, and Storage

The **memory hierarchy** in a computer system is a structured arrangement of different types of memory, each with its own speed, cost, and size characteristics. This hierarchy optimizes performance by ensuring that the fastest and most expensive memory is used for frequently accessed data, while slower, cheaper memory provides storage for less frequently used information. Understanding the relationship between cache, RAM, and storage is key to grasping how computers achieve efficient data processing.

At the top of the hierarchy is **cache memory**, the fastest and most expensive type of memory in a system. Cache resides directly on the processor chip or very close to it, making it accessible within just a few clock cycles. Its primary purpose is to store copies of frequently accessed data and instructions, reducing the time the processor spends retrieving them from slower memory. Cache is typically divided into levels: **L1 (Level 1)**, **L2 (Level 2)**, and **L3 (Level 3)**.

L1 cache is the smallest but fastest, often split into separate caches for instructions and data. For example, a modern processor might have a 32 KB L1 instruction cache and a 32 KB L1 data cache per core. L2 cache is larger, usually shared across cores, and slightly slower, serving as a secondary buffer. L3 cache, shared among all cores in a multi-core processor, is the largest but also the slowest within the cache hierarchy. Despite its slower speed compared to L1 and L2, L3 cache is still much faster than main memory (RAM).

Cache operates on the principle of locality, which includes **temporal locality** and **spatial locality**. Temporal locality means that recently accessed data is likely to be accessed again soon, so cache retains this data for quick access. Spatial locality implies that data near recently accessed memory locations is also likely to be accessed, encouraging the storage of contiguous blocks of data in cache. These principles ensure that cache optimally reduces the number of slow memory accesses.

The **cache replacement policy** determines which data in the cache is replaced when the cache is full. Common policies include **Least Recently Used (LRU)**, which evicts the least recently accessed data, and **First-In-First-Out (FIFO)**, which removes the oldest data. The choice of policy impacts the efficiency of cache operations and varies depending on the workload.

Below the cache in the memory hierarchy is **Random Access Memory (RAM)**, also called main memory. RAM is a type of volatile memory, meaning it loses its contents when the power is turned off. It serves as the workspace for the processor, holding data and instructions for active processes. Modern systems typically use **DDR (Double Data Rate) SDRAM**, with newer generations like DDR4 and DDR5 offering higher speeds and lower power consumption.

RAM's speed is measured in nanoseconds, significantly slower than cache but still much faster than storage devices. For example, accessing data in RAM might take 50–70 nanoseconds, compared to just a few nanoseconds for L1 cache. RAM is organized into **memory modules**, such as DIMMs (Dual Inline Memory Modules), which are installed on the motherboard. The capacity of RAM in modern computers ranges from a few gigabytes for low-end systems to hundreds of gigabytes in high-performance servers.

Memory access patterns significantly affect performance. Sequential access, where data is read or written in order, is faster than random access because it aligns with the prefetching mechanisms of RAM and cache. To optimize memory usage, modern processors employ techniques like **memory interleaving**, which spreads data across multiple memory modules to allow parallel access and increase throughput.

Below RAM in the hierarchy is **secondary storage**, which provides long-term, non-volatile data storage. Secondary storage devices include **hard disk drives (HDDs)**, **solid-state drives (SSDs)**, and **hybrid drives**. HDDs use spinning magnetic disks to store data, making them slower but more affordable for large capacities. Access times for HDDs are measured in milliseconds, much slower than RAM or cache, because of mechanical delays in moving the read/write head to the correct position on the disk.

SSDs, in contrast, use **NAND flash memory**, offering much faster access times since there are no moving parts. SSDs access data in microseconds, bridging the gap between RAM and traditional HDDs in the hierarchy. Modern SSDs, particularly those using the **NVMe (Non-Volatile Memory Express)** interface, can achieve data transfer speeds of several gigabytes per second, making them ideal for high-performance applications like gaming, video editing, and data analytics.

Hybrid drives combine the benefits of HDDs and SSDs by including a small amount of SSD storage as a cache for frequently accessed data. This design provides a cost-effective way to improve performance while maintaining large storage capacities. For example, a hybrid drive might store an operating system and frequently used applications in its SSD cache, while less frequently accessed files remain on the HDD portion.

The memory hierarchy also includes **tertiary storage** for archival purposes, such as optical disks (CDs, DVDs) and magnetic tapes. These storage media are much slower and are typically used for backup and long-term data storage rather than active use. Cloud storage services, while technically part of tertiary storage, are gaining prominence for their accessibility and scalability.

Another layer in the hierarchy is **virtual memory**, which extends the usable memory space by using a portion of the storage drive as temporary RAM. The operating system manages virtual memory using **paging**, dividing memory into fixed-size blocks called pages. When RAM is full, less frequently accessed pages are moved to a **swap file** on the storage drive. While this increases the apparent memory capacity, accessing data in virtual memory is much slower than accessing data in physical RAM.

Latency and bandwidth are two critical factors that influence the performance of the memory hierarchy. Latency measures the time it takes to access data, while bandwidth refers to the amount of data that can be transferred in a given period. Cache has the lowest latency and highest bandwidth, followed by RAM, and then secondary storage. Efficient memory hierarchies aim to minimize latency for critical operations while maximizing bandwidth for data-intensive tasks.

Prefetching and caching strategies help bridge the performance gap between different levels of the hierarchy. Prefetching anticipates future data needs and loads data into faster memory levels before it is explicitly requested. For example, a processor might prefetch data from RAM into cache while executing a program loop, ensuring that subsequent iterations have immediate access to required data.

Modern systems also use **memory controllers** to optimize communication between the processor and memory. Memory controllers manage tasks like refreshing DRAM, handling memory requests, and implementing error correction through **ECC (Error-Correcting Code)**. Integrated memory controllers, now common in processors like Intel's Core and AMD's Ryzen, reduce latency by eliminating the need for a separate chipset.

The **hierarchical design** ensures that the most critical and frequently used data resides in the fastest memory, while less frequently accessed data is stored in slower, larger-capacity storage. This layered approach balances cost, performance, and capacity, enabling computers to handle a wide range of applications effectively.

Primary vs. Secondary Storage

Primary storage and **secondary storage** are essential components of a computer's memory system, each serving distinct roles in data processing and storage. Understanding the differences between them involves examining their speed, volatility, and function within the memory hierarchy.

Primary storage, often referred to as **main memory**, is the workspace for the processor. It is **volatile memory**, meaning it loses all stored data when the system is powered off. **Random Access Memory (RAM)** is the most common type of primary storage, providing fast and temporary storage for data and instructions that the CPU is actively using. RAM operates at speeds measured in nanoseconds, making it orders of magnitude faster than secondary storage devices like hard drives or SSDs.

Primary storage is designed for **high-speed access**. The processor can directly retrieve or write data to RAM without intermediaries, allowing for real-time processing. For instance, when you open a file or run a program, the data is loaded from secondary storage into RAM. This ensures that the processor can access the necessary information quickly, avoiding the delays associated with slower secondary storage devices.

The **limited capacity** of RAM, typically ranging from a few gigabytes in low-end systems to hundreds of gigabytes in servers, restricts the amount of data it can store. This limitation necessitates the use of secondary storage for long-term data retention. Additionally, primary storage's volatile nature makes it unsuitable for storing critical information that must persist after the system is powered down.

Secondary storage is **non-volatile memory**, meaning it retains data even when the power is turned off. Devices like **hard disk drives (HDDs)**, **solid-state drives (SSDs)**, and **optical disks** fall into this category. Unlike RAM, which is used for active processes, secondary storage is responsible for long-term data storage, including the operating system, applications, and user files.

Secondary storage is significantly slower than primary storage due to its reliance on mechanical components (in the case of HDDs) or slower electronic interfaces (in the case of SSDs). For example, a typical HDD has an access time measured in milliseconds, while SSDs, though faster, still lag behind RAM with access times in microseconds. However, secondary storage compensates for this slower speed with its **high capacity**. HDDs commonly offer terabytes of storage, while SSDs, though more expensive, are increasingly available in large capacities.

One key difference between primary and secondary storage lies in their **cost per bit**. RAM is more expensive to manufacture due to its speed and design, making it impractical for storing large amounts of data. Secondary storage, particularly HDDs, offers a lower cost per bit, making it economical for bulk storage.

The relationship between primary and secondary storage is dynamic. When a system is in operation, data and programs are transferred from secondary storage to primary storage as needed. This process is managed by the operating system, which prioritizes which data remains in RAM based on usage patterns. For instance, frequently used files or applications may stay in primary storage, while less-used data resides in secondary storage until required.

In modern systems, the introduction of **caches** and **hybrid storage solutions** has blurred the lines between primary and secondary storage. For example, **NVMe SSDs** offer speeds close to RAM in certain applications, while hybrid drives combine the capacity of HDDs with a small cache of SSD storage to improve performance. These technologies aim to reduce the performance gap between primary and secondary storage, enhancing system responsiveness.

While primary storage is essential for immediate access and processing, secondary storage ensures **data persistence and scalability**. Together, they create a balance between speed, cost, and capacity, supporting the complex demands of modern computing systems.

Virtual Memory Concepts

Virtual memory is a key concept in modern computing that extends the usable memory space beyond the physical limits of a system's **primary storage (RAM)**. By using a portion of the secondary storage as an extension of RAM, virtual memory enables a computer to run larger programs and handle more processes simultaneously than would otherwise be possible.

The operating system manages virtual memory through a process called **paging**. Memory is divided into fixed-size blocks called **pages**, typically 4 KB in size. When a program's data or instructions exceed the available physical RAM, the operating system moves some of these pages to a reserved area on the secondary storage, known as the **page file** or **swap file**. This allows the program to continue running as if the system has more RAM than it physically does.

The transfer of pages between RAM and the page file is known as **swapping**. When the processor needs data that resides in virtual memory, the operating system retrieves the required page from secondary storage and places it back in RAM. This process is called a **page fault**, and it introduces significant delays since accessing data from secondary storage is much slower than accessing it from RAM. However, careful management of virtual memory minimizes the frequency and impact of page faults.

Virtual memory enables **multitasking** by allowing multiple programs to share the available physical memory. Each program is given its own virtual address space, creating the illusion that it has access to a large, contiguous block of memory. This isolation enhances security and stability, preventing one program from interfering with the memory of another.

The concept of **virtual addressing** underpins virtual memory. The processor generates virtual addresses for data and instructions, which the **memory management unit (MMU)** translates into physical addresses in RAM or the page file. This abstraction simplifies programming by allowing developers to work with a uniform address space without worrying about the underlying hardware configuration.

One challenge of virtual memory is the **overhead introduced by paging and swapping**. Frequent page faults, known as **thrashing**, occur when the system spends more time moving data between RAM and the page file than executing programs. Thrashing degrades performance and can render the system unresponsive. To mitigate thrashing, modern operating systems use techniques like **working sets**, which prioritize keeping the most frequently accessed pages in physical memory.

Page replacement algorithms determine which pages to move out of RAM when new pages need to be loaded. Common algorithms include **Least Recently Used (LRU)**, which replaces the page that has not been used for the longest time, and **First-In-First-Out (FIFO)**, which evicts the oldest page in memory. These algorithms aim to minimize page faults by predicting usage patterns.

Virtual memory also supports advanced features like **memory protection** and **address space layout randomization (ASLR)**. Memory protection prevents unauthorized access to specific memory regions, enhancing system security. ASLR randomizes the location of key data structures in memory, making it harder for attackers to exploit vulnerabilities.

The performance of virtual memory depends on the speed of the **secondary storage** used for the page file. Systems with SSDs benefit from faster virtual memory performance compared to those with HDDs. However, even SSDs cannot match the speed of physical RAM, making efficient memory management critical.

Modern operating systems often combine virtual memory with other techniques like **memory compression**. Compression reduces the size of inactive data in RAM, allowing more data to stay in physical memory and reducing reliance on the slower page file. This approach balances performance and resource utilization in memory-constrained environments.

Virtual memory transforms how computers manage resources, enabling systems to handle complex workloads and large datasets seamlessly. It acts as a bridge between limited physical memory and the demands of modern software, making efficient use of available hardware.

Solid-State Drives (SSD) vs. Hard Disk Drives (HDD)

Solid-state drives (SSDs) and **hard disk drives (HDDs)** are two primary types of secondary storage devices used in computing systems. Each has unique characteristics, architectures, and performance profiles, making them suitable for different applications.

Understanding their differences involves examining their design, speed, durability, cost, and use cases.

An **HDD** is a mechanical storage device that uses magnetic disks, known as platters, to store data. The platters spin at high speeds while a read/write head, mounted on an actuator arm, moves across the disk's surface to access or record data. The operation of an HDD relies on **magnetic storage principles**, where data is stored as magnetized regions on the platters. These regions represent binary data (0s and 1s), and the read/write head senses or alters these magnetic states.

An **SSD**, on the other hand, uses **flash memory** to store data. It has no moving parts and relies on semiconductor-based NAND flash cells to store binary information. Flash memory is non-volatile, meaning it retains data even when the power is turned off. SSDs use a controller to manage data storage, retrieval, and wear leveling, ensuring efficient performance and prolonged lifespan.

The most noticeable difference between SSDs and HDDs is **speed**. HDDs have relatively slow access times due to their mechanical nature. The read/write head must physically move to the correct position on the spinning platter before data can be accessed, introducing latency. The average latency for an HDD is measured in milliseconds, typically around 4–12 ms depending on the drive's RPM (revolutions per minute). Common HDDs spin at 5400 or 7200 RPM, while high-performance models for enterprise use may reach 10,000 or 15,000 RPM. In contrast, SSDs have no moving parts, enabling near-instantaneous data access. Their latency is measured in microseconds—often 100 times faster than HDDs. This speed advantage makes SSDs particularly suited for tasks requiring rapid data retrieval, such as booting operating systems, running applications, or handling high-resolution video editing.

Data transfer rates further highlight this difference. HDDs generally achieve transfer speeds of 80–160 MB/s for consumer-grade drives, while high-performance models can reach around 250 MB/s. SSDs, depending on their interface, can far exceed these speeds. **SATA-based SSDs**, the older standard, typically offer speeds up to 550 MB/s, while **NVMe SSDs**, which use the PCIe interface, achieve transfer rates of 2–7 GB/s or higher. This dramatic difference in throughput makes SSDs the clear choice for performance-critical applications.

Durability is another key distinction. The mechanical components in an HDD make it vulnerable to physical shocks, vibrations, and wear over time. Dropping an HDD or subjecting it to harsh conditions can cause the read/write head to crash into the platter, resulting in permanent data loss. SSDs, lacking moving parts, are far more robust in such scenarios. They can withstand greater physical impact and are better suited for portable devices like laptops and external drives that experience frequent movement.

However, SSDs are not immune to wear. Their **NAND flash memory** cells degrade slightly each time data is written to or erased from them. This phenomenon, known as **write endurance**, limits the number of write cycles each cell can handle. Modern SSDs mitigate this through **wear leveling**, a technique that spreads write operations evenly across all cells to maximize the drive's lifespan. Manufacturers rate SSD durability using metrics like **TBW (terabytes written)** or **DWPD (drive writes per day)**, providing an estimate of how much data can be written before the drive becomes unreliable. For typical consumer use, SSDs are designed to last several years, and advancements in technology continue to improve their endurance.

Capacity is a factor where HDDs still maintain an advantage. HDDs are available in much larger capacities at a lower cost per gigabyte, making them ideal for applications requiring extensive storage, such as backups, video archives, or data centers. Consumer-grade HDDs often come in capacities of 1–8 TB, with enterprise models reaching 20 TB or more. SSDs, while catching up, remain more expensive for similar capacities. Affordable SSDs for consumers typically range from 256 GB to 2 TB, though higher-capacity models are becoming increasingly common.

The **cost per gigabyte** significantly differentiates the two. HDDs are much cheaper, with prices often below $0.03 per GB for high-capacity models. SSDs, particularly NVMe drives, cost several times more, though the gap is narrowing as production scales and manufacturing processes improve. For cost-sensitive applications requiring bulk storage, HDDs remain the preferred choice, while SSDs are chosen for performance-critical scenarios.

The **power consumption** of SSDs is generally lower than that of HDDs. HDDs require power to spin their platters and move the actuator arm, consuming 5–10 watts during operation. SSDs, in contrast, typically consume 2–5 watts, depending on the model and workload. This lower power consumption makes SSDs more suitable for battery-powered devices like laptops or embedded systems, where energy efficiency is critical.

The **form factors** of SSDs and HDDs also differ. HDDs are typically available in 3.5-inch and 2.5-inch sizes, with the larger form factor used in desktops and servers, and the smaller one in laptops and portable drives. SSDs offer greater flexibility, coming in 2.5-inch drives compatible with SATA interfaces, as well as compact **M.2** and **U.2** form factors designed for PCIe and NVMe interfaces. The small size of M.2 SSDs enables them to fit into ultrabooks, tablets, and even IoT devices without sacrificing performance.

In terms of **heat generation and noise**, SSDs outperform HDDs. HDDs produce heat due to friction between mechanical parts and generate audible noise during operation, especially under heavy workloads. SSDs, being solid-state devices, operate silently and produce minimal heat, contributing to better overall thermal management in systems.

When it comes to **data recovery**, HDDs have an edge in some cases. Data stored magnetically on platters can often be retrieved by professionals even if the drive experiences hardware failure. SSDs, however, pose greater challenges for recovery due to their use of **TRIM commands** and garbage collection, which permanently erase data blocks to maintain performance. Once data is deleted from an SSD, it is usually unrecoverable, making regular backups critical for users relying on SSDs.

The **environmental impact** of both devices is another consideration. SSDs are more energy-efficient and lighter, reducing transportation and operational energy costs. However, their production involves complex manufacturing processes and rare materials, which have a higher environmental cost compared to HDDs. HDDs, with their mechanical components, are easier to recycle but consume more energy during use, especially in large-scale deployments.

In hybrid systems, SSDs and HDDs often work together to balance speed and capacity. For example, an SSD can serve as the boot drive, hosting the operating system and frequently accessed programs, while an HDD provides bulk storage for files, backups, or less frequently used applications. This setup leverages the strengths of both storage types, offering a cost-effective way to improve overall system performance without sacrificing storage capacity.

The choice between SSDs and HDDs depends on the specific use case. SSDs dominate where speed, durability, and energy efficiency are paramount, such as in laptops, gaming systems, and enterprise servers handling high-frequency transactions. HDDs, on the other hand, excel in applications requiring massive storage at a low cost, such as archival systems, media servers, and backup solutions.

The evolution of storage technology continues to blur the lines between SSDs and HDDs. Emerging solutions like **QLC (quad-level cell) NAND SSDs** offer higher capacities at reduced costs, encroaching on the traditional domain of HDDs. Conversely, advancements in HDD technology, such as **HAMR (heat-assisted magnetic recording)** and **SMR (shingled magnetic recording)**, aim to push HDD capacities even further while improving efficiency.

Despite their differences, both SSDs and HDDs remain indispensable in modern computing, complementing each other in a wide range of applications. Whether prioritizing performance, capacity, or cost, understanding the strengths and limitations of each technology ensures optimal storage solutions for diverse needs.

CHAPTER 6: OPERATING SYSTEMS AND SYSTEM SOFTWARE

Functions and Components of Operating Systems

An **operating system (OS)** is the backbone of any computer system, managing hardware resources and providing an interface between users and the machine. It acts as a bridge, enabling applications to communicate effectively with hardware while ensuring the efficient allocation of resources. To understand how an operating system works, it is essential to break it down into its functions and components, each of which addresses a specific aspect of system management.

One of the primary functions of an operating system is **process management**. A process is an instance of a running program, and the OS ensures that multiple processes can coexist and execute efficiently. It uses **scheduling algorithms** to decide which process runs at any given time, balancing CPU usage among all active tasks. For example, a round-robin scheduler allocates time slices to each process in a cyclic order, while priority scheduling allows more critical processes to run first. The OS also manages process states—new, ready, running, waiting, and terminated—ensuring smooth transitions between these states as a program executes.

Closely related to process management is **multitasking**, which enables multiple processes to run concurrently. Multitasking can be preemptive, where the OS forcibly switches between tasks, or cooperative, where tasks yield control voluntarily. Preemptive multitasking ensures responsiveness, especially in real-time systems, by interrupting low-priority tasks to handle time-sensitive operations. This functionality is critical for modern applications, where multiple programs, like a web browser, music player, and document editor, run simultaneously.

The OS also handles **memory management**, ensuring that programs have the memory they need to execute while preventing conflicts. It keeps track of memory allocation using structures like page tables and segment tables. Virtual memory, a feature managed by the OS, extends physical memory by using disk space to simulate additional RAM. When a program's data exceeds available RAM, the OS moves less frequently used data to a **swap file** on the disk, retrieving it later as needed. This process, called **paging**, allows systems to run large applications even with limited physical memory.

Another critical function is **file system management**, which governs how data is stored, organized, and accessed on storage devices. The file system provides a logical structure for data, organizing it into files and directories regardless of the underlying physical storage medium. Common file systems include **NTFS**, **FAT32**, **ext4**, and **APFS**, each optimized for different use cases. The OS manages file creation, deletion, reading, writing, and permissions, ensuring data integrity and security. For instance, it prevents unauthorized users from accessing sensitive files through access control mechanisms.

The **I/O management** component oversees input and output devices like keyboards, mice, printers, and network adapters. The OS uses device drivers—software that translates between hardware instructions and application commands—to standardize communication with different devices. For example, when a user presses a key on a keyboard, the OS processes this input and routes it to the appropriate application. It also buffers I/O operations, temporarily storing data to smooth out disparities in device speeds.

Resource allocation is another core responsibility of an OS. Resources like the CPU, memory, storage, and peripheral devices are limited, and the OS ensures they are distributed fairly among processes. This involves detecting resource conflicts and resolving them through mechanisms like deadlock prevention and recovery. Deadlocks occur when multiple processes are stuck waiting for resources held by each other, halting system progress. The OS employs strategies like resource ordering or timeouts to prevent such scenarios.

User management is a critical function, particularly in multi-user systems. The OS authenticates users, authorizes access to resources, and enforces security policies. For instance, a server running a multi-user operating system like Linux allows multiple users to log in simultaneously, each with specific permissions and access rights. The OS isolates users' activities, ensuring that one user's actions do not interfere with another's.

The **kernel** is the central component of the operating system, responsible for managing hardware interactions and providing core system services. It operates at the lowest level, directly interfacing with the CPU, memory, and I/O devices. Kernels come in different designs, such as monolithic kernels, where all core functionalities are integrated into a single large program, and microkernels, which minimize the kernel's size by delegating most services to user-space processes. While monolithic kernels like those in Linux provide high performance, microkernels prioritize modularity and fault isolation.

The OS also includes a **shell**, which serves as the interface between users and the system. A shell can be command-line-based, like Bash in Linux, or graphical, like Windows Explorer. It interprets user commands, passes them to the kernel, and returns the results. For instance, typing `ls` in a Linux terminal lists the contents of a directory, while clicking an icon in a graphical shell opens a file or application.

In addition to core management tasks, modern operating systems incorporate **security features** to protect data and resources. They implement authentication mechanisms like passwords, biometrics, or multi-factor authentication to verify user identities. They also enforce process isolation, preventing malicious software from accessing memory or files belonging to other applications. Firewalls, encryption, and secure boot mechanisms further enhance the system's defense against threats.

Networking capabilities are another key feature of modern operating systems. The OS manages **network protocols**, such as TCP/IP, to enable communication between devices on a network. This involves assigning IP addresses, handling data packets, and ensuring reliable data transfer. For instance, when a user sends an email, the OS breaks the data into packets, routes them to the destination, and reassembles them upon arrival.

Operating systems also provide **application programming interfaces (APIs)**, enabling developers to build software that interacts seamlessly with hardware and system resources. These APIs simplify complex tasks like file handling, memory allocation, and network communication, allowing developers to focus on application logic. For example, the Windows API includes functions for creating windows, managing threads, and accessing files.

Another component of an OS is the **scheduler**, which determines the order in which tasks are executed. The scheduler's efficiency directly impacts system performance, particularly in environments with high computational demands. For instance, a real-time operating system (RTOS) uses deterministic scheduling algorithms to guarantee that critical tasks meet their deadlines, making it suitable for applications like industrial automation and robotics.

Error detection and handling are integral to the OS's functionality. Hardware failures, software bugs, and invalid user inputs can disrupt system operations. The OS detects such errors, logs them, and takes corrective actions. For instance, if a program attempts to access invalid memory, the OS generates a **segmentation fault** and terminates the program to prevent further issues.

Virtualization support is a feature of many modern operating systems, allowing multiple virtual machines to run on a single physical machine. Virtualization enables better resource utilization and provides isolation between different workloads. Hypervisors, either embedded in the OS or running as standalone software, manage these virtual machines by allocating resources and ensuring their independence from each other.

Power management is another critical aspect, particularly for mobile and energy-efficient devices. The OS reduces power consumption by putting unused components into low-power states or adjusting CPU frequency based on workload demands. For example, modern operating systems implement features like sleep mode, hibernation, and dynamic voltage scaling to optimize energy use without compromising performance.

An OS also includes diagnostic tools and utilities that help users monitor and maintain the system. Tools like task managers, disk defragmenters, and system logs provide insights into resource usage, performance bottlenecks, and errors. These utilities assist both end users and administrators in troubleshooting issues and optimizing system operations.

Process Management and Scheduling

Process management is a core function of an operating system (OS), ensuring that multiple processes can execute efficiently and share system resources without interference. A **process** is an instance of a program in execution, containing its code, data, and the state necessary to run. The OS manages processes by creating, executing, suspending, and terminating them while coordinating their interactions with system resources.

When a program is initiated, the OS creates a corresponding process, assigning it a unique **process identifier (PID)**. The process is then placed into one of several **states**: new, ready, running, waiting, or terminated. The new state indicates that the process is being initialized, while the ready state signifies that it is prepared to execute but is waiting for the CPU. A process in the running state is actively executing instructions, whereas a waiting process is idle, awaiting the completion of an I/O operation or another event. The OS transitions processes between these states as they execute, ensuring smooth multitasking.

The **Process Control Block (PCB)** is a critical data structure maintained by the OS to track the status of each process. The PCB contains information such as the PID, process state, program counter (address of the next instruction), CPU registers, memory allocation details, and resource usage statistics. The OS updates the PCB as the process transitions through various states, ensuring that it can resume execution without loss of data or progress.

Scheduling determines the order in which processes access the CPU and other resources. This ensures that all processes are given fair access while optimizing overall system performance. Scheduling is divided into three levels: **long-term scheduling, medium-term scheduling**, and **short-term scheduling**.

Long-term scheduling decides which processes are admitted into the system for execution. It controls the degree of multiprogramming, determining how many processes can be in memory at a given time. For instance, in a batch processing system, the long-term scheduler selects jobs from a queue and loads them into memory based on resource availability.

Medium-term scheduling focuses on swapping processes in and out of memory to manage resource contention and optimize system performance. When the system becomes overloaded, the medium-term scheduler suspends less critical processes, freeing up memory and CPU cycles for higher-priority tasks. These suspended processes are stored in secondary storage and reloaded when resources become available.

Short-term scheduling, also known as CPU scheduling, determines which ready process gets the CPU next. The **CPU scheduler** operates at a much higher frequency than the other schedulers, making decisions every few milliseconds or microseconds. It selects a process from the ready queue based on a defined scheduling algorithm, preempting the current process if necessary.

Scheduling algorithms are categorized as **preemptive** or **non-preemptive**. In preemptive scheduling, the CPU can be taken away from a process before it completes its execution. Non-preemptive scheduling allows a process to run until it finishes or voluntarily releases the CPU. Each approach has its own use cases and trade-offs.

First-Come, First-Served (FCFS) is a simple non-preemptive scheduling algorithm where processes are executed in the order they arrive. While straightforward, FCFS suffers from the **convoy effect**, where a long-running process delays subsequent processes, leading to poor average turnaround time.

Shortest Job Next (SJN) selects the process with the shortest expected execution time. It minimizes average turnaround time but is not practical for real-time systems because it requires prior knowledge of process durations. Its preemptive variant, **Shortest Remaining Time First (SRTF)**, interrupts the current process if a shorter process arrives.

Round-Robin (RR) is a preemptive algorithm widely used in time-sharing systems. It assigns a fixed time slice, or **quantum**, to each process in the ready queue. When a process's quantum expires, it is moved to the back of the queue, and the next process is given the CPU. RR ensures responsiveness and fairness but requires careful tuning of the quantum to balance throughput and latency.

Priority Scheduling assigns a priority level to each process and selects the highest-priority process for execution. This can be preemptive or non-preemptive. While effective for systems with processes of varying importance, priority scheduling can lead to **starvation**, where low-priority processes are indefinitely delayed. To mitigate this, the OS may implement **aging**, gradually increasing the priority of long-waiting processes.

Multilevel Queue Scheduling divides processes into separate queues based on their priority or type (e.g., interactive, batch, real-time). Each queue has its own scheduling algorithm, and the OS allocates CPU time among the queues based on predefined policies. For example, interactive processes might have higher priority and shorter time slices, ensuring quick responsiveness.

Multilevel Feedback Queue Scheduling extends multilevel queues by allowing processes to move between queues based on their execution history. For instance, a process that consumes excessive CPU time may be demoted to a lower-priority queue, while an I/O-bound process may be promoted for faster execution. This dynamic adjustment improves overall system efficiency and fairness.

Context switching occurs when the CPU switches from one process to another. During a context switch, the OS saves the current process's state in its PCB and loads the state of the next process. While necessary for multitasking, context switching introduces overhead because saving and restoring states consumes CPU cycles. Minimizing unnecessary context switches is crucial for maintaining system performance.

Process synchronization is another critical aspect of process management, ensuring that multiple processes can cooperate without conflict. In systems with shared resources, the OS prevents **race conditions**, where two or more processes attempt to access the same resource simultaneously, leading to unpredictable results. Synchronization mechanisms like **semaphores**, **mutexes**, and **monitors** enforce mutual exclusion, ensuring that only one process can access a critical section at a time.

The OS also handles **inter-process communication (IPC)**, enabling processes to exchange data and coordinate their actions. IPC mechanisms include **message passing**, where processes send and receive messages, and **shared memory**, where processes communicate by reading and writing to a common memory space. For example, a producer-consumer problem might use a shared buffer to synchronize data production and consumption, with semaphores controlling access to the buffer.

Deadlock prevention and recovery are integral to process management. A deadlock occurs when a group of processes becomes stuck, each waiting for resources held by another. The OS employs strategies like resource ordering, where processes must request resources in a specific sequence, or the **banker's algorithm**, which allocates resources only if it ensures system safety. If a deadlock does occur, the OS may terminate one or more processes to break the cycle and free resources.

Modern operating systems also support **thread management**, where a process is divided into smaller units of execution called threads. Threads within the same process share memory and resources, allowing for lightweight multitasking. For instance, a web browser might use separate threads for rendering pages, handling user input, and managing network requests. The OS manages thread scheduling alongside process scheduling, ensuring efficient execution of both.

Memory Management

Memory management is one of the most critical functions of an operating system (OS). It ensures that programs have the memory they need to execute while optimizing the utilization of available memory resources. By managing memory effectively, the OS allows multiple programs to run simultaneously without conflicts, making multitasking and resource sharing possible. This process involves allocation, deallocation, and monitoring of memory in real-time.

The operating system divides memory into two primary sections: **kernel space** and **user space**. Kernel space is reserved for the OS itself, ensuring it can execute its functions without interference. User space, on the other hand, is allocated to applications and processes. This separation maintains system stability by isolating user programs from the sensitive operations of the kernel.

A fundamental aspect of memory management is **address translation**, which maps logical addresses used by programs to physical addresses in the system's hardware. This translation is handled by the **Memory Management Unit (MMU)**, a hardware component integrated into the processor. The MMU uses data structures like page tables to keep track of these mappings, enabling seamless access to memory while maintaining isolation between processes.

Memory is allocated in units called **pages** or **segments**, depending on the memory management scheme. **Paging** is a widely used technique where memory is divided into fixed-size blocks called pages. The logical address space of a process is split into pages, which are mapped to physical memory frames. Pages do not need to be contiguous in memory, allowing for efficient utilization of fragmented memory. For example, a 4 KB page can reside in any available 4 KB frame, regardless of its location in physical memory.

Segmentation, in contrast, divides memory into variable-sized segments based on the logical structure of a program, such as code, data, and stack. Each segment is assigned a unique identifier, and its size reflects the program's needs. Segmentation aligns more closely with the logical organization of programs but can lead to external fragmentation, where free memory is scattered in non-contiguous blocks.

The OS uses **virtual memory** to extend the apparent size of RAM by leveraging secondary storage, such as a hard drive or SSD. Virtual memory creates the illusion of a larger memory space, allowing systems to run programs that exceed the physical RAM capacity. The OS swaps less frequently used data from RAM to a **swap file** or **page file** on the storage device, retrieving it when needed. This process, known as **paging**, enables efficient use of limited physical memory but introduces latency when accessing data from slower storage.

The use of virtual memory introduces challenges such as **page faults**, which occur when a program accesses data not currently in physical memory. When a page fault happens, the OS retrieves the missing page from the storage device and loads it into RAM. Frequent page faults, a condition known as **thrashing**, degrade system performance, as the OS spends more time swapping pages than executing programs. To mitigate thrashing, the OS uses **working set models** to keep frequently accessed pages in memory.

Page replacement algorithms determine which page to evict from memory when new pages need to be loaded. Common algorithms include **Least Recently Used (LRU)**, which removes the page that has not been accessed for the longest time, and **First-In-First-Out (FIFO)**, which evicts the oldest page in memory. These algorithms aim to minimize page faults by predicting access patterns and optimizing memory usage.

In systems with multiple processes, the OS enforces **memory isolation** to ensure that one process cannot access the memory of another. This isolation is achieved through address translation and permission settings managed by the MMU. If a process attempts to access unauthorized memory, the OS generates a **segmentation fault** and terminates the process to protect system integrity.

Another key concept in memory management is **dynamic allocation**, where memory is allocated to programs during runtime based on their needs. This contrasts with static allocation, where memory is assigned at compile time. Dynamic allocation is more flexible but requires efficient management to prevent fragmentation and leaks. **Malloc** and **free** in C, or **new** and **delete** in C++, are examples of functions that enable dynamic memory allocation in programming languages.

Fragmentation is a significant challenge in memory management. **External fragmentation** occurs when free memory is scattered in small, non-contiguous blocks, making it difficult to allocate large blocks despite having sufficient total free memory. **Internal fragmentation** happens when allocated memory blocks are larger than required, leaving unused space within them. To address fragmentation, the OS employs techniques like **compaction**, which consolidates free memory into contiguous regions, or **buddy allocation**, which splits memory into power-of-two blocks to simplify allocation and reduce fragmentation.

Memory management also includes **cache management**, where frequently accessed data is stored in fast, small caches closer to the CPU. The OS ensures that cache contents are synchronized with main memory, using policies like **write-through** or **write-back** to maintain consistency. Efficient cache management reduces memory latency and enhances system performance.

Memory protection mechanisms safeguard critical data and system stability. For example, the OS uses **read-only** and **execute-only** permissions to prevent processes from modifying or executing unauthorized memory regions. These protections are enforced at the hardware level by the MMU and supported by the OS's memory management software.

Modern operating systems support **shared memory**, allowing multiple processes to access the same memory region. Shared memory is commonly used in **inter-process communication (IPC)**, enabling fast data exchange between cooperating processes. However, the OS must implement synchronization mechanisms like **semaphores** or **mutexes** to prevent data corruption and ensure consistency.

Memory allocation policies also have a role in system performance. The OS decides whether to allocate memory in a **first-fit, best-fit**, or **worst-fit** manner. First-fit allocates the first block of memory large enough for the request, while best-fit searches for the smallest suitable block, and worst-fit uses the largest available block. Each approach has trade-offs in terms of speed and fragmentation.

For high-performance applications, memory management includes features like **huge pages** and **non-uniform memory access (NUMA)**. Huge pages reduce the overhead of managing small page sizes, while NUMA optimizes memory access in multi-processor systems by placing memory closer to the processor that accesses it most frequently.

Operating systems also incorporate **memory compression** to make efficient use of RAM. Compressed pages are stored in memory instead of being swapped to disk, reducing I/O latency and improving performance. This feature is particularly useful in resource-constrained systems or environments with high memory demand.

Security in memory management is critical, especially in modern systems exposed to threats like **buffer overflows** and **memory-based attacks**. The OS enforces techniques such as **Address Space Layout Randomization (ASLR)**, which randomizes the location of key memory regions, making it harder for attackers to predict their addresses. Additionally, **Data Execution Prevention (DEP)** prevents code from executing in non-executable memory regions, mitigating certain types of exploits.

The operating system's ability to handle **real-time memory demands** is essential in systems with strict timing requirements, such as industrial automation or embedded devices. Real-time operating systems (RTOS) allocate memory deterministically, ensuring predictable performance. They also use static allocation and avoid paging to meet stringent latency constraints.

Virtualization introduces additional complexity in memory management. Virtual machines share physical memory, and the hypervisor oversees allocation across guest operating systems. Techniques like **memory deduplication** identify and merge identical memory pages across virtual machines, reducing redundant usage. **Ballooning** allows guest OSs to release unused memory back to the hypervisor for redistribution, enhancing efficiency.

The evolution of memory management continues with advances like **persistent memory (PMEM)**, which combines the speed of RAM with the persistence of storage. PMEM enables faster recovery from system crashes and reduces the reliance on traditional storage devices. Operating systems are adapting to support these new memory technologies, ensuring seamless integration into existing architectures.

Effective memory management is the cornerstone of a reliable and efficient operating system, balancing the competing demands of processes, applications, and system stability. By using advanced algorithms and hardware-supported mechanisms, the OS ensures optimal utilization of memory resources, enabling complex systems to operate smoothly.

File Systems and Storage Management

File systems and **storage management** are fundamental aspects of operating systems, enabling the organization, storage, retrieval, and management of data on storage devices. These components provide the abstraction necessary for users and applications to interact with physical storage without worrying about hardware complexities. The operating system ensures data integrity, optimizes performance, and enforces security through its file system and storage management mechanisms.

A **file system** organizes data into logical units called files. Files are collections of related data, and the file system assigns them a name, type, and metadata, such as size, permissions, and timestamps. This metadata is stored in the **file system's directory structure**, which acts as an index to locate files on the storage device. Directories, in turn, are hierarchical containers that organize files into a tree-like structure, allowing for intuitive navigation and management.

Operating systems support various **file system types**, each optimized for specific use cases. For example, **NTFS (New Technology File System)**, used by Windows, supports large file sizes, journaling for data integrity, and advanced access control. In contrast, **ext4 (Fourth Extended File System)**, a default in many Linux distributions, emphasizes performance and scalability. Other systems, like **FAT32**, offer broad compatibility but lack advanced features, making them suitable for portable devices like USB drives.

Storage devices are divided into **blocks**, fixed-size units that serve as the smallest unit of data storage. The file system maps logical file data to these physical blocks. When a file is created or extended, the OS allocates a series of blocks to store its contents. Efficient block allocation is critical to prevent fragmentation and ensure optimal performance. Two common block allocation strategies are **contiguous allocation**, where blocks are stored sequentially, and **linked allocation**, where blocks are scattered across the disk but linked via pointers.

Fragmentation is a challenge in file systems, occurring when data is scattered across non-contiguous blocks. Fragmentation slows down data access as the storage device's read/write head must jump to multiple locations to retrieve a file. The OS combats fragmentation using **defragmentation tools**, which reorganize blocks to restore sequential order, and through allocation strategies that minimize fragmentation from the outset.

Journaling file systems add another layer of reliability. In these systems, changes to the file system are logged in a journal before being applied. If a crash or power failure occurs, the journal ensures that incomplete updates are rolled back or completed, preserving data integrity. NTFS and ext4, for instance, use journaling to protect against corruption during unexpected interruptions.

Storage management extends beyond individual file systems, encompassing how the OS interacts with storage devices, allocates space, and handles redundancy. Storage devices include **hard disk drives (HDDs)**, **solid-state drives (SSDs)**, and network-based systems like **SANs (Storage Area Networks)**. The OS abstracts the specifics of these devices, presenting a uniform interface for applications to access and manage data.

Modern storage solutions often incorporate **logical volume management (LVM)**, allowing storage to be dynamically allocated and resized without interrupting system operation. LVM creates logical volumes that sit atop physical storage devices, enabling flexible partitioning, data mirroring, and striping. For example, an LVM system can combine multiple physical drives into a single logical volume, simplifying storage management and improving performance.

The OS manages storage hierarchies through **mount points**, which associate file systems with specific directories in the system's directory tree. For instance, a secondary storage drive might be mounted at `/data`, making its contents accessible under that directory. Mounting allows seamless integration of multiple storage devices, regardless of their physical locations or formats.

Disk quotas are another feature of storage management, restricting the amount of space a user or group can consume. Quotas prevent individual users from monopolizing storage resources, ensuring fair usage. The OS tracks disk usage and enforces these limits, generating alerts or denying further writes when quotas are exceeded.

Caching is a key mechanism in storage management, bridging the speed gap between storage devices and the processor. The OS caches frequently accessed data in faster memory, such as RAM, to reduce latency. For instance, when a file is read from disk, its contents are cached so that subsequent accesses are served directly from memory. This reduces the need for repeated disk reads and improves performance.

RAID (Redundant Array of Independent Disks) is commonly used to enhance storage reliability and performance. RAID configurations combine multiple physical drives into a single logical unit, distributing or duplicating data across them. For example, RAID 0 stripes data across drives for increased performance, while RAID 1 mirrors data for redundancy. Higher RAID levels, like RAID 5 and RAID 6, combine these approaches, offering both performance and fault tolerance. The OS works in conjunction with hardware or software RAID controllers to manage these arrays.

The OS also enforces **file permissions** to regulate access to files and directories. Permissions determine who can read, write, or execute a file, providing a basic layer of security. In Linux, for instance, permissions are defined for the owner, group, and others, using attributes such as r (read), w (write), and x (execute). Advanced file systems like NTFS offer more granular permissions through **Access Control Lists (ACLs)**, allowing specific permissions for individual users or groups.

In addition to managing individual devices, operating systems support **networked file systems**, enabling remote storage access. Protocols like **NFS (Network File System)** and **SMB (Server Message Block)** allow files on a remote server to appear as though they are stored locally. This abstraction simplifies file sharing across networks and is widely used in enterprise environments. For example, an organization might use NFS to provide shared directories for team collaboration.

Backup and recovery mechanisms are integral to file system and storage management. The OS integrates with backup utilities to create snapshots or archives of critical data, ensuring it can be restored in the event of hardware failure, accidental deletion, or corruption. Incremental backups, which save only the changes since the last backup, minimize storage overhead and backup time. Some file systems, like ZFS, include native snapshot capabilities, allowing point-in-time recovery with minimal effort.

As storage capacities grow, file systems must support **large volumes** and **big files** efficiently. For example, NTFS supports individual file sizes up to 16 exabytes, while ext4 can handle volumes as large as 1 exabyte. File systems designed for specialized purposes, such as **HDFS (Hadoop Distributed File System)**, scale across thousands of nodes, enabling storage and analysis of petabyte-scale datasets.

Data integrity is another critical aspect of storage management. File systems like **ZFS** and **btrfs** include **checksumming** to detect and correct data corruption. Checksums are calculated when data is written to storage and verified during read operations. If corruption is detected, redundant copies of the data are used to restore the original content, ensuring reliability.

The OS also handles **encryption** to protect sensitive data. File systems like **APFS** and NTFS support transparent encryption, where data is encrypted and decrypted on the fly without user intervention. Encryption keys are securely stored, and access is restricted to authorized users, safeguarding data against unauthorized access even if the storage device is stolen.

For systems with diverse storage needs, **tiered storage** strategies optimize performance and cost. Frequently accessed data is stored on fast but expensive SSDs, while infrequently accessed data resides on slower, cheaper HDDs or archival storage like tape drives. The OS monitors access patterns and automatically migrates data between tiers, ensuring efficient utilization of resources.

Emerging technologies, such as **non-volatile memory express (NVMe)** and **persistent memory**, are transforming storage management. NVMe SSDs leverage high-speed PCIe interfaces for unprecedented performance, while persistent memory combines the speed of RAM with the durability of traditional storage. Operating systems are adapting to these advancements, introducing features like direct access (DAX) for ultra-low-latency storage operations.

File systems and storage management also incorporate **log-structured designs**, where all writes are appended to a log rather than modifying existing data in place. This approach minimizes write amplification and improves performance, especially on SSDs, which have limited write endurance. Log-structured file systems like **F2FS** are designed specifically for flash storage, optimizing data placement and garbage collection.

CHAPTER 7: PROGRAMMING FOUNDATIONS

How Code/Software Interacts with Hardware

Code bridges the gap between human intentions and machine actions. It transforms high-level instructions written by developers into operations that a computer's hardware can execute. This interaction is made possible through layers of abstraction, starting with high-level programming languages, moving through compilers and operating systems, and ending with the physical actions of transistors inside the hardware.

At the top layer, programmers write code in **high-level languages** like Python, Java, or C++. These languages are designed to be human-readable, abstracting away the complexities of hardware. A simple statement like `print("Hello, World!")` in Python instructs the computer to display text on the screen. However, this command must go through several translation steps before the hardware understands it.

The first step in this journey involves **compilers** or **interpreters**, which convert high-level code into **machine code**, a series of binary instructions the processor can execute. A compiler translates the entire program into machine code before execution, while an interpreter translates and executes code line by line. For instance, in the C programming language, a compiler converts a loop like `for (int i = 0; i < 10; i++)` into a sequence of binary instructions that control how the processor manages memory, updates registers, and compares values.

The machine code generated by the compiler is tailored to the **instruction set architecture (ISA)** of the processor. The ISA defines the basic operations a processor can perform, such as arithmetic operations, data transfers, and branching. Common ISAs include x86, ARM, and RISC-V. A command in machine code might instruct the processor to add two numbers stored in registers or move data from memory to a specific register.

Assembly language serves as a bridge between high-level code and machine code. While still low-level, assembly language is human-readable, using mnemonics like MOV, ADD, or JMP to represent operations. For example, the assembly instruction ADD AX, BX tells the processor to add the contents of register BX to register AX. Programmers working on performance-critical applications or embedded systems often use assembly to optimize specific operations, but most modern development relies on higher-level languages.

Once the machine code is prepared, the operating system (OS) takes over. The OS acts as an intermediary, ensuring that software and hardware interact seamlessly. For instance, when a program needs to read data from a file, it sends a **system call** to the OS. The OS handles the low-level details, such as interacting with the file system, locating the data on the storage device, and transferring it to memory. This abstraction allows developers to write code without worrying about hardware specifics.

After the OS processes the request, the machine code is loaded into **memory** and executed by the **processor (CPU)**. The CPU follows the **fetch-decode-execute cycle** to process each instruction. First, the processor fetches the next instruction from memory, as specified by the **program counter (PC)**. It then decodes the instruction to determine what operation is required, such as arithmetic or data movement. Finally, it executes the instruction, updating registers, memory, or output devices as needed.

The **registers** within the CPU are a key part of this process. Registers are small, high-speed memory locations used to store intermediate values, such as the operands for a calculation or the result of a comparison. For example, when adding two numbers, the CPU might load them into registers AX and BX, perform the addition, and store the result back into AX. Registers ensure that the processor can access critical data without delays caused by fetching it from main memory.

Memory management is another critical aspect of software-hardware interaction. Programs use **RAM (Random Access Memory)** to store data and instructions during execution. The OS allocates memory for each process, ensuring that they don't interfere with one another. The memory management unit (MMU) translates the logical addresses used by programs into physical addresses in RAM, maintaining isolation and security. For instance, when a program accesses a variable, the MMU ensures that the corresponding memory location is correctly identified and accessed.

Hardware devices like **keyboards, mice, and displays** interact with software through **device drivers**, which are specialized programs that translate high-level commands into hardware-specific instructions. For example, when you press a key, the keyboard driver converts the electrical signal from the keypress into a format the OS can understand. Similarly, a graphics driver translates commands from a game or application into instructions that control the GPU, rendering images on the screen.

The interaction between software and hardware extends to **input/output (I/O) operations**, which are managed through **I/O ports** and **buses**. When a program writes data to a file, the OS sends the data through an I/O bus to the storage device. Conversely, when the program reads input from a sensor, the data flows from the sensor to the processor via the same I/O pathways. These operations are synchronized with **interrupts**, signals that inform the processor when a device is ready for communication or needs attention.

Peripheral devices like printers, scanners, and network cards rely on protocols to standardize communication with the system. For example, a printer uses USB or

Ethernet protocols to receive data from the OS. The OS ensures that the printer receives data in the correct format, enabling it to produce the desired output.

Multithreading and parallelism optimize how software utilizes hardware resources. Modern processors have multiple cores, each capable of executing its own thread. When a program is designed to handle multiple threads, such as downloading a file while processing user input, the OS distributes these threads across available cores. This parallel execution increases efficiency, allowing software to take full advantage of the processor's capabilities.

The interaction between code and hardware also involves **power management**. The OS adjusts the CPU's clock speed and voltage based on workload, reducing energy consumption when demand is low. For instance, during idle periods, the processor enters low-power states, suspending certain operations while maintaining responsiveness.

Networking adds another layer of complexity to software-hardware interaction. When a program sends data over a network, it passes the data to the OS, which encapsulates it in packets using protocols like TCP/IP. The OS then transmits these packets through the network interface card (NIC) to the physical network. On the receiving end, the NIC processes incoming packets and forwards them to the OS, which reassembles them for the application.

Graphics processing is an area where software leverages specialized hardware. Modern GPUs (Graphics Processing Units) execute parallel operations on large datasets, making them ideal for rendering images and running machine learning algorithms. Software uses APIs like OpenGL or DirectX to communicate with the GPU, specifying tasks like drawing a 3D object or applying a texture. The GPU translates these instructions into operations on its processing cores, delivering high-performance graphics rendering.

In embedded systems, the relationship between software and hardware is even more direct. These systems often bypass operating systems, with programs interacting directly with hardware registers and peripherals. For example, a microcontroller controlling a robotic arm might execute assembly instructions to move the arm to a specific position, reading sensor data to ensure precise movements.

Firmware, a type of low-level software embedded in hardware, further illustrates this interaction. Firmware controls hardware behavior at the most basic level, from initializing components during startup to managing low-level operations. For instance, the BIOS/UEFI firmware initializes the hardware during boot and hands control over to the OS once the system is ready.

The interaction between software and hardware continues to evolve with technologies like **virtualization** and **cloud computing**. Virtual machines use hypervisors to abstract hardware resources, allowing multiple operating systems to share the same physical hardware. Cloud platforms distribute software across vast networks of servers, with each server's hardware abstracted from the application layer.

Introduction to Programming Paradigms

A **programming paradigm** is a style or methodology of programming that defines how developers write and structure code. Paradigms shape the way problems are thought about and solved in software development, influencing everything from how data is represented to how tasks are executed. By understanding programming paradigms, developers can choose the best tools and approaches for their projects, leading to clearer, more efficient, and maintainable code.

One of the oldest and most widely used paradigms is **procedural programming**, which focuses on organizing code into sequences of instructions or procedures. These procedures, also called functions, perform specific tasks and can be reused throughout a program. Procedural programming follows a step-by-step approach where the program's flow is controlled by loops, conditionals, and function calls. Languages like C, Pascal, and Fortran are examples of procedural programming languages. For instance, in C, a program to calculate the sum of an array might involve writing a `for` loop inside a function, ensuring that each step is explicitly defined and executed in order.

In procedural programming, data and functions are typically separate. This separation means that functions act on data structures passed to them as arguments. While this approach is straightforward, it can become unwieldy in large programs where data and functions that operate on it are closely related. This limitation paved the way for paradigms that offered a more structured way to model real-world systems.

Object-oriented programming (OOP) emerged to address some of these challenges by treating everything in a program as an object. Objects are self-contained entities that combine data and the functions (or methods) that operate on that data. This paradigm mirrors real-world concepts, making it intuitive for modeling complex systems. For example, in a program simulating a school, objects like `Student` and `Teacher` might have properties (e.g., name, age) and methods (e.g., takeExam, teachClass). Languages like Java, Python, C++, and Ruby support OOP, emphasizing concepts such as **encapsulation**, **inheritance**, and **polymorphism**.

Encapsulation binds data and methods together within an object, protecting internal details from external interference. For instance, an object's data can be marked private, making it accessible only through specific methods. This control ensures that data integrity is maintained. **Inheritance** allows a class to inherit properties and methods from another class, promoting code reuse. For example, a `Vehicle` class might provide general attributes like speed and methods like move, while specific classes like `Car` or

78

`Bike` inherit these features and add their own. **Polymorphism** enables methods to behave differently depending on the object that calls them. A common example is method overriding, where a subclass redefines a method from its parent class to suit its specific needs.

While OOP is highly effective for many applications, it is not always the best fit for tasks like data processing, simulations, or algorithm-heavy programs. For these, **functional programming** offers a powerful alternative. Functional programming treats computation as the evaluation of mathematical functions, avoiding changes to state and mutable data. This paradigm emphasizes immutability and pure functions, which always produce the same output for the same input without side effects.

Languages like Haskell, Scala, and Lisp are dedicated functional programming languages, while others like Python, JavaScript, and C# incorporate functional features. A key concept in functional programming is **higher-order functions**, which can accept other functions as arguments or return them as results. For example, in Python, the `map` function applies a given function to each item in a list, creating a new list of results. A developer might use `map` to double every number in a list with a simple one-line expression.

Recursion is another hallmark of functional programming, where functions call themselves to solve problems incrementally. For instance, calculating the factorial of a number can be elegantly expressed as a recursive function: `factorial(n) = n * factorial(n-1)`. This approach contrasts with the iterative loops commonly found in procedural code. Functional programming also heavily relies on **lambda expressions** or anonymous functions, allowing concise definitions of simple operations without naming them explicitly.

Logic programming is a paradigm that defines programs as sets of logical statements, relying on inference to deduce results. Instead of specifying how to achieve a goal, logic programming focuses on what the goal is. Prolog is the most prominent language in this paradigm. For instance, in Prolog, defining a family tree involves specifying relationships like parent and child, and the system can infer more complex relationships such as grandparent or cousin by applying logical rules. Logic programming is particularly well-suited for tasks like natural language processing, expert systems, and problem-solving where constraints and relationships are central.

Another important paradigm is **declarative programming**, where developers describe the desired results without explicitly detailing the steps to achieve them. Functional and logic programming are subsets of declarative programming, but the term also encompasses paradigms like **database query languages** (e.g., SQL). In SQL, querying a database to find all employees earning more than $50,000 involves a single declarative statement: `SELECT * FROM employees WHERE salary > 50000;`. The database engine handles the details of how to retrieve the data, abstracting away the procedural complexity.

Event-driven programming is yet another paradigm, commonly used in applications with graphical user interfaces (GUIs), games, or real-time systems. This paradigm revolves around responding to events such as user input, sensor signals, or messages from other systems. In event-driven programming, the flow of the program is determined by events and their associated handlers. For instance, in JavaScript, clicking a button might trigger a function that validates form data or updates a webpage. The **callback functions** and **event listeners** central to this paradigm allow developers to create highly interactive and dynamic applications.

Concurrent and parallel programming focus on executing multiple tasks simultaneously, taking advantage of multi-core processors and distributed systems. These paradigms are essential for applications like real-time simulations, web servers, and large-scale data processing. **Concurrency** involves managing multiple tasks that can start, run, and complete in overlapping time periods. For example, a web server might handle multiple client requests concurrently. **Parallel programming**, in contrast, divides a task into smaller parts that run simultaneously on different processors, such as splitting a large dataset across multiple cores for faster computation.

Languages and frameworks like Java, Go, and MPI (Message Passing Interface) support concurrent and parallel programming through constructs like **threads**, **goroutines**, and **process pools**. Developers often use synchronization mechanisms such as **locks**, **semaphores**, and **message queues** to coordinate these tasks and avoid conflicts like race conditions.

Reactive programming is a relatively newer paradigm, focusing on asynchronous data streams and changes over time. It is particularly useful in scenarios where systems must react to real-time updates, such as stock market applications or social media feeds. Reactive programming frameworks like **RxJS** and **React** allow developers to define how the system should respond to changes in data, ensuring responsiveness and scalability.

While each paradigm has unique strengths, many modern programming languages adopt a **multi-paradigm** approach, combining features from multiple paradigms. For instance, Python supports procedural, object-oriented, and functional programming, allowing developers to choose the style that best suits their problem. Similarly, JavaScript supports both event-driven and functional programming, making it versatile for web development.

Programming paradigms continue to evolve, influenced by advances in hardware, software, and the growing complexity of modern applications. Each paradigm offers a distinct lens for approaching problems, encouraging developers to think critically about their tools and techniques.

Basics of High-Level Programming Languages

High-level programming languages are designed to be more readable and accessible to humans compared to low-level assembly or machine code. They abstract away the complexities of hardware, allowing developers to focus on solving problems rather than managing the intricacies of memory addresses, CPU instructions, and register usage. These languages provide a bridge between human thought and machine execution, empowering programmers to create complex systems with relative ease.

High-level languages use **syntax and semantics** that are closer to natural language, often supplemented with mathematical notations and keywords. For example, Python uses simple, human-readable keywords like `if`, `for`, and `while`, making code intuitive even for beginners. This design contrasts with assembly language, where operations rely on mnemonics like `MOV` or `ADD` and require detailed knowledge of hardware architecture.

One of the defining features of high-level languages is **portability**. Unlike low-level languages, which are tightly coupled to specific hardware, high-level languages are designed to run on multiple platforms. This is achieved through compilers or interpreters, which translate high-level code into machine code tailored for the target hardware. For example, Java achieves platform independence by compiling code into bytecode, which is executed by the Java Virtual Machine (JVM) on any platform.

High-level languages typically provide **data types and structures** that simplify the organization and manipulation of data. Primitive data types like integers, floats, characters, and booleans are fundamental building blocks, while more complex structures like arrays, lists, dictionaries, and classes enable the creation of sophisticated systems. For example, a high-level language like Python allows developers to store and manipulate a list of customer names using simple syntax: `customers = ["Alice", "Bob", "Charlie"]`. This abstraction eliminates the need to manually allocate and manage memory for these structures.

Another key characteristic of high-level languages is their use of **control structures** to define the flow of execution. Conditional statements like `if-else`, loops like `for` and `while`, and functions enable developers to write logical, modular, and reusable code. These constructs allow programs to make decisions, iterate over data, and perform repetitive tasks efficiently. For example, iterating through a list in Python to print each element requires a simple loop:

```
for customer in customers: print(customer)
```

Functions are a cornerstone of high-level programming, enabling developers to encapsulate blocks of code that perform specific tasks. Functions take input parameters, process them, and return results, promoting **code reuse** and modularity. For instance, a function to calculate the square of a number in JavaScript might look like this: `function square(num) { return num * num; }`.
Functions make code easier to read, debug, and maintain, as changes to functionality can be made in a single location rather than multiple occurrences throughout the program.

High-level languages often include built-in **libraries and frameworks**, which provide pre-written code for common tasks like file handling, network communication, and graphical user interfaces. For example, Python's `math` library offers functions for complex mathematical operations, while JavaScript's DOM manipulation APIs enable developers to dynamically modify web pages. These libraries save time and effort, allowing developers to focus on application logic rather than reinventing the wheel.

Error handling is another essential feature of high-level programming languages. Most languages provide mechanisms like **try-catch blocks** to detect, report, and manage errors gracefully. For instance, in Python, a developer can handle potential errors in file operations as follows:

```
try: file = open("data.txt", "r") except FileNotFoundError:
print("File not found.")
```

This approach prevents unexpected crashes and improves the robustness of applications. Memory management is largely automated in high-level languages, reducing the burden on developers. Many languages include **garbage collection**, which automatically reclaims memory that is no longer in use. For example, in Java, the garbage collector runs periodically to identify and clean up objects that are no longer referenced. This automation minimizes memory leaks and ensures efficient utilization of system resources.

High-level languages support **object-oriented programming (OOP)** principles, such as encapsulation, inheritance, and polymorphism. These features enable developers to model real-world entities as objects, making code more intuitive and aligned with the problem domain. For example, in Java, a `Car` class might define properties like `make` and `model` and methods like `start()` and `stop()`. Individual car objects can then be created from this class, each with its own unique attributes.

Many high-level languages also offer **functional programming features**, such as lambda functions, map-reduce operations, and immutability. These features are particularly useful for processing collections of data and writing concise, declarative code. For instance, in Python, doubling the elements of a list can be accomplished with a single line:

```
doubled = list(map(lambda x: x * 2, numbers))
```

Such functional programming constructs are ideal for data-driven applications and parallel computing.

Interactivity is a significant strength of high-level languages, especially in environments like **interpreted languages**. Languages like Python and JavaScript allow developers to run code line-by-line in interactive shells or consoles, making it easier to test and debug small snippets of code. This feature is invaluable for rapid prototyping and learning, as developers can experiment with different approaches without the overhead of compiling and running entire programs.

High-level languages are often equipped with **type systems** to enforce rules about how data can be used. **Static typing**, found in languages like C++ and Java, requires developers to explicitly declare variable types, reducing runtime errors. For example, int age = 25; ensures that the variable age can only store integer values. On the other hand, **dynamic typing**, used in Python and JavaScript, allows variables to hold any type of data, offering flexibility but requiring careful runtime checks. Both approaches have their advantages, depending on the application and developer preferences.

Concurrency and parallelism are increasingly supported in high-level languages to leverage modern multi-core processors. Constructs like **threads**, **async/await**, and **goroutines** enable programs to execute multiple tasks simultaneously or asynchronously. For example, in JavaScript, asynchronous operations like fetching data from an API are handled with promises:

```
fetch(url).then(response => response.json()).then(data =>
console.log(data));
```

These features enhance performance and responsiveness in applications like web servers, real-time systems, and data processing pipelines.

The evolution of high-level programming languages has led to the emergence of **domain-specific languages (DSLs)** tailored for specific tasks. For example, SQL is designed for database queries, HTML for structuring web pages, and MATLAB for numerical computing. These languages provide concise syntax and specialized tools, making them ideal for their intended domains while remaining easy to integrate with general-purpose languages.

Debugging tools are integral to high-level programming environments, enabling developers to identify and resolve issues efficiently. Integrated Development Environments (IDEs) like Visual Studio, PyCharm, and Eclipse provide features like **breakpoints**, **step-through debugging**, and **variable inspection**. These tools allow developers to pause program execution at specific points, examine the state of variables, and understand the flow of logic.

High-level languages also emphasize **cross-platform compatibility**, enabling applications to run on various operating systems and devices with minimal modifications. For instance, Java's "write once, run anywhere" philosophy relies on the JVM to ensure that Java applications work consistently across different platforms. Similarly, web technologies like HTML, CSS, and JavaScript are inherently cross-platform, functioning seamlessly on any browser.

Compilation vs. Interpretation

Compilation and **interpretation** are two fundamental approaches to translating high-level programming languages into machine-readable instructions that can be executed by a computer. Both methods enable software to run on hardware, but they differ significantly in how they process code, their performance characteristics, and their use cases. Understanding these differences is critical to choosing the right programming tools and optimizing software development.

In **compilation**, the entire program is translated into machine code before execution. This process involves a **compiler**, which reads the source code, analyzes it for syntax and semantic correctness, and generates an executable file. This file contains low-level instructions tailored to the target system's hardware architecture, such as x86 or ARM. For example, in a C program, the gcc compiler translates the code into an executable binary. Once compiled, the program can be executed directly by the operating system without requiring the compiler or source code.

Compilation typically follows multiple stages, including **lexical analysis**, **syntax analysis**, **semantic analysis**, **intermediate code generation**, and **optimization**. During lexical analysis, the compiler breaks the source code into tokens, such as keywords, identifiers, and operators. Syntax analysis constructs a **parse tree** to ensure the code follows the grammar rules of the programming language. Semantic analysis verifies logical consistency, such as type compatibility. Intermediate code generation creates a low-level, machine-independent representation of the program, which is then optimized for performance before being converted into machine code.

One of the main advantages of compilation is its **performance**. Since the machine code is generated in advance, the program does not need to be translated during runtime, leading to faster execution. For example, compiled languages like C, C++, and Go are often chosen for performance-critical applications such as operating systems, game engines, and embedded systems. Additionally, compiled programs are more secure since the source code is not exposed at runtime, making it harder for users to reverse-engineer the logic.

However, compilation has some downsides. The compilation process can be time-consuming, especially for large programs, as it involves analyzing and translating the entire codebase. Any changes to the source code require recompilation, which can slow down the development cycle. Furthermore, compiled programs are typically platform-specific, meaning they must be recompiled for each target architecture, such as Windows, macOS, or Linux.

Interpretation, on the other hand, translates and executes code line by line during runtime. An **interpreter** reads the source code, translates each instruction into machine code, and executes it immediately. For instance, when running a Python script, the Python interpreter processes each line of code dynamically. This eliminates the need for a separate compilation step and allows developers to test and debug code interactively.

The dynamic nature of interpretation makes it highly flexible and well-suited for **rapid prototyping** and **scripting tasks**. Languages like Python, JavaScript, and Ruby are interpreted, enabling developers to experiment with code, modify it, and see the results instantly. This is particularly useful in environments like data analysis, web development, and interactive applications, where quick iterations are essential.

Despite its flexibility, interpretation comes with performance limitations. Since the code is translated during runtime, interpreted programs are slower than compiled ones. Each instruction must be processed repeatedly, introducing overhead that can be significant for computationally intensive tasks. For example, a loop in an interpreted language must translate and execute the same line of code multiple times, whereas a compiled program performs the loop directly in machine code.

Interpreted languages often support features like **dynamic typing**, where variable types are determined at runtime. This allows for greater flexibility but introduces runtime checks that further impact performance. For instance, in Python, a variable can change types dynamically (`x = 5; x = "hello"`), and the interpreter ensures that each operation is valid for the current type. While convenient, this feature contrasts with statically typed, compiled languages like C, where type errors are caught during compilation.

Hybrid approaches combine compilation and interpretation to balance performance and flexibility. For example, **Java** programs are first compiled into **bytecode**, an intermediate, platform-independent representation. This bytecode is then interpreted or just-in-time (JIT) compiled by the Java Virtual Machine (JVM) at runtime. Similarly, languages like Python and JavaScript use **JIT compilation** in modern implementations to improve performance by converting frequently executed code paths into machine code during runtime.

The distinction between compilation and interpretation also affects how errors are detected and handled. In compiled languages, errors are typically caught during the compilation phase, preventing the program from running until all issues are resolved. This early detection ensures that compiled programs are free of syntax and semantic errors before execution. In contrast, interpreted languages detect errors at runtime, meaning the program may partially execute before encountering an issue. While this allows for faster development cycles, it can lead to unpredictable behavior if errors are not thoroughly tested beforehand.

Compilation often provides better **optimization** opportunities since the compiler has access to the entire codebase before execution. Compilers use advanced optimization techniques like **loop unrolling**, **inlining functions**, and **register allocation** to improve performance. For example, inlining replaces a function call with its actual code, eliminating the overhead of jumping to another memory location. These optimizations make compiled programs highly efficient, particularly for large-scale systems.

In contrast, interpreters prioritize **portability** and ease of use over optimization. Interpreted programs are inherently platform-independent, as the interpreter handles the specifics of the underlying hardware. For instance, a Python script can run on any system with a Python interpreter installed, regardless of the operating system or architecture. This portability makes interpreted languages ideal for applications like web development, where code must run seamlessly across diverse environments.

The choice between compilation and interpretation often depends on the **use case** and **development priorities**. For applications requiring high performance, tight resource constraints, or long-term deployment, compiled languages are preferred. Examples include real-time systems, high-performance computing, and embedded devices. On the other hand, for tasks requiring rapid development, frequent updates, or cross-platform compatibility, interpreted languages are more suitable.

The evolution of programming languages has blurred the lines between compilation and interpretation. Many modern languages, like C# and Python, employ intermediate representations to achieve a balance of performance, portability, and flexibility. For instance, Python code is first compiled into bytecode, which is then interpreted by the Python runtime. Similarly, .NET languages compile into an intermediate language (IL), which is executed by the Common Language Runtime (CLR).

Understanding the trade-offs between compilation and interpretation helps developers choose the right tools for their projects and optimize their workflows. Both methods have unique strengths, and their coexistence reflects the diverse needs of modern programming environments.

CHAPTER 8: ALGORITHMS AND DATA STRUCTURES

Key Algorithms in Computer Science

Algorithms are step-by-step procedures for solving problems or performing tasks. They are the foundation of computer science, powering everything from search engines to navigation systems. Understanding key algorithms is essential for designing efficient solutions to computational problems. These algorithms are categorized by their purpose, such as sorting, searching, graph traversal, and optimization.

Sorting algorithms organize data into a specified order, such as ascending or descending. One of the simplest sorting algorithms is **Bubble Sort**, where adjacent elements are compared and swapped if they are in the wrong order. The process repeats until the list is sorted. While easy to understand, Bubble Sort is inefficient for large datasets, with a time complexity of $O(n^2)$.

Merge Sort, on the other hand, is more efficient and uses a divide-and-conquer approach. The algorithm splits the list into smaller sublists until each contains a single element, then merges these sublists back together in sorted order. With a time complexity of $O(n \log n)$, Merge Sort is faster than Bubble Sort for large datasets, though it requires additional memory for merging.

Another efficient sorting algorithm is **Quick Sort**, which also follows a divide-and-conquer strategy. It selects a "pivot" element, partitions the list into two sublists based on whether elements are smaller or larger than the pivot, and recursively sorts these sublists. Quick Sort's average-case time complexity is $O(n \log n)$, but it can degrade to $O(n^2)$ if the pivot is poorly chosen, such as in a list that is already sorted.

Searching algorithms locate specific elements within a dataset. **Linear Search** is the simplest approach, where each element is checked one by one until the target is found or the list is exhausted. While intuitive, Linear Search has a time complexity of $O(n)$, making it inefficient for large datasets.

Binary Search is a more efficient algorithm for sorted lists. It repeatedly divides the search interval in half, eliminating half of the remaining elements at each step. For example, to search for a number in a sorted array, the algorithm compares the target with the middle element. If the target is smaller, it searches the left half; if larger, the right half. Binary Search has a time complexity of $O(\log n)$, making it much faster than Linear Search for large datasets.

Graph algorithms solve problems involving networks of nodes and edges, such as finding the shortest path or detecting cycles. **Breadth-First Search (BFS)** explores all nodes at the current depth level before moving to the next level. Starting from a given node, BFS visits its neighbors, marking each as visited, and proceeds until all reachable nodes are explored. BFS is often used for finding the shortest path in unweighted graphs, as it guarantees that the first time a node is reached, it is via the shortest route.

Depth-First Search (DFS) takes a different approach, exploring as far down a branch as possible before backtracking. DFS is implemented using recursion or a stack and is particularly useful for problems like detecting cycles or finding connected components in a graph. Both BFS and DFS have a time complexity of $O(V + E)$, where V is the number of vertices and E is the number of edges.

Dijkstra's Algorithm is a graph algorithm designed to find the shortest path between nodes in a weighted graph. Starting from a source node, it maintains a priority queue to explore the nearest unvisited nodes, updating their distances if a shorter path is found. Dijkstra's Algorithm is widely used in navigation systems and network routing, with a time complexity of $O((V + E) \log V)$ when implemented with a binary heap.

Another important algorithm for shortest paths is the **Bellman-Ford Algorithm**, which handles graphs with negative edge weights. Unlike Dijkstra's, Bellman-Ford can detect negative weight cycles. It relaxes all edges repeatedly, updating the shortest path estimates for each vertex. While slower, with a time complexity of $O(VE)$, it is more versatile for graphs with unusual edge weights.

Kruskal's Algorithm and **Prim's Algorithm** are used to find the **Minimum Spanning Tree (MST)** of a graph. An MST connects all nodes in a graph with the smallest possible total edge weight, ensuring no cycles. Kruskal's Algorithm sorts all edges by weight and adds them to the MST in ascending order, as long as they don't form a cycle. Prim's Algorithm, in contrast, starts from a single node and grows the MST by adding the smallest edge that connects a new node. Both algorithms have a time complexity of $O(E \log E)$, as sorting or maintaining a priority queue dominates their execution.

Dynamic programming is a method for solving problems by breaking them into overlapping subproblems and storing the results of these subproblems to avoid redundant computation. One classic example is the **Fibonacci sequence**, where each term is the sum of the two preceding terms. A naive recursive solution recalculates the same subproblems repeatedly, leading to exponential time complexity. By storing intermediate results in a table, dynamic programming reduces the time complexity to $O(n)$.

Another famous dynamic programming problem is the **Knapsack Problem**, which involves selecting items with given weights and values to maximize value without exceeding a weight limit. Using a table to store the maximum value achievable for each weight limit, the algorithm builds solutions incrementally. This approach has a time complexity of O(nW), where n is the number of items and W is the weight limit.

Divide-and-conquer algorithms split problems into smaller subproblems, solve them independently, and combine their results. **Binary Search**, **Merge Sort**, and **Quick Sort** are examples of divide-and-conquer algorithms. A more advanced example is the **Fast Fourier Transform (FFT)**, which efficiently computes the discrete Fourier transform of a sequence, reducing its time complexity from $O(n^2)$ to $O(n \log n)$. FFT is essential in fields like signal processing and image compression.

Greedy algorithms make decisions step by step, always choosing the option that seems best at the moment. While not always optimal, greedy algorithms work well for problems like **Huffman Coding**, which generates an optimal binary tree for data compression. By repeatedly combining the two smallest elements into a new node, Huffman Coding ensures the most frequently used symbols have the shortest codes, minimizing the overall size of encoded data.

Backtracking algorithms explore all possible solutions to a problem by building them incrementally and abandoning paths that fail to meet constraints. The **N-Queens Problem** is a classic example, where the goal is to place N queens on an N×N chessboard such that no two queens threaten each other. Backtracking systematically places queens and undoes moves when conflicts arise, ensuring all valid arrangements are found.

Sorting and searching algorithms, **graph traversal methods**, **dynamic programming**, and **greedy techniques** are just the tip of the iceberg. These algorithms provide the building blocks for solving complex computational problems efficiently.

Fundamental Data Structures: Arrays, Lists, Trees

Arrays, **lists**, and **trees** are foundational data structures in computer science, each suited for specific use cases and operations. They provide the framework for organizing and accessing data efficiently, forming the building blocks for many algorithms and advanced structures.

An **array** is a collection of elements stored in contiguous memory locations, where each element is accessed using its index. Arrays are ideal for situations where data size is fixed and direct access to elements is critical. For instance, accessing the 10th element in an array requires a single calculation: base address + (index × size of element). This constant time access, O(1), makes arrays highly efficient for retrieval operations. However, their fixed size can be a limitation. Resizing an array requires allocating a new block of memory and copying the data, which is time-consuming and inefficient for dynamic datasets.

In contrast, **linked lists** provide flexibility in managing data size. A linked list consists of nodes, where each node contains a data value and a pointer to the next node in the sequence. Linked lists come in several types, including **singly linked lists**, **doubly linked lists**, and **circular linked lists**. In a singly linked list, traversal is unidirectional, starting from the head node. Doubly linked lists, with pointers to both the next and previous nodes, allow bidirectional traversal, making operations like deletion and insertion more efficient in certain cases. Circular linked lists connect the last node back to the first, creating a loop structure. While accessing elements in a linked list is slower (O(n)), since traversal is sequential, dynamic resizing and efficient insertion or deletion make them suitable for situations like implementing queues or stacks.

A **tree** is a hierarchical data structure consisting of nodes, where each node has a parent and potentially multiple children. Trees are used to represent data with a natural hierarchy, such as file systems or organizational structures. A **binary tree**, the most common type, restricts each node to at most two children, typically labeled as left and right. Binary trees are efficient for searching and sorting when balanced, as they offer O(log n) performance for insertions, deletions, and lookups.

Binary Search Trees (BSTs) are a specialized type of binary tree where the left child contains values less than the parent, and the right child contains values greater than the parent. This structure ensures that in-order traversal produces sorted output. However, unbalanced BSTs, such as those formed by inserting already sorted data, degrade to linked lists, reducing their efficiency to O(n).

To maintain balance, **self-balancing binary trees** like **AVL trees** and **Red-Black trees** are used. AVL trees enforce strict balance by ensuring that the height difference between the left and right subtrees of any node is at most one. Red-Black trees, on the other hand, allow some imbalance but enforce properties that ensure logarithmic time operations. These trees are widely used in database indexing and memory management.

Heaps are another form of tree structure, specifically designed for efficient priority management. A **min-heap** ensures that the smallest element is always at the root, while a **max-heap** ensures the largest element is at the root. Heaps are fundamental to algorithms like **Heapsort** and are used in priority queues, where the highest or lowest priority element must be accessed quickly.

Sorting and Searching Techniques

Sorting and searching techniques are essential for organizing and retrieving data efficiently. These operations improve the performance of many algorithms, enabling faster access, manipulation, and decision-making.

Sorting algorithms vary in complexity and use cases. **Bubble Sort** is a simple, comparison-based algorithm where adjacent elements are swapped if they are out of order. This process repeats until the array is sorted. While Bubble Sort is easy to implement, its $O(n^2)$ time complexity makes it impractical for large datasets. For example, sorting 1,000 elements might require up to 1,000,000 comparisons, making it inefficient in real-world scenarios.

Insertion Sort improves upon Bubble Sort for nearly sorted datasets. It works by dividing the array into a sorted and unsorted region. Starting with the first element as the sorted region, it inserts each subsequent element into its correct position within the sorted region. Insertion Sort performs well for small or partially sorted datasets, with an average time complexity of $O(n^2)$ but near $O(n)$ in favorable cases.

For more scalable sorting, **Merge Sort** is an efficient divide-and-conquer algorithm. It splits the array into halves, recursively sorts each half, and then merges them into a sorted whole. With a time complexity of $O(n \log n)$, Merge Sort is well-suited for large datasets but requires additional memory for merging, which can be a drawback in memory-constrained environments.

Quick Sort is another divide-and-conquer algorithm, known for its speed and efficiency in practice. It selects a "pivot" element, partitions the array into two groups based on the pivot, and recursively sorts the partitions. While its average-case time complexity is $O(n \log n)$, poorly chosen pivots can lead to $O(n^2)$ performance. Strategies like random pivot selection mitigate this risk, making Quick Sort a common choice in standard library implementations.

Heap Sort combines the efficiency of heaps with sorting. The algorithm builds a max-heap from the data, then repeatedly extracts the maximum element, placing it at the end of the array. With a time complexity of $O(n \log n)$ and no additional memory requirements, Heap Sort is an excellent choice for memory-efficient sorting.

For searching, **Linear Search** is the most straightforward technique, examining each element sequentially. While it works on both sorted and unsorted datasets, its $O(n)$ time complexity makes it inefficient for large collections. For example, finding a single element in a dataset of 1,000 items might require checking every item in the worst case.

Binary Search, designed for sorted datasets, reduces the search space by half at each step. Starting with the middle element, it determines whether the target is smaller, larger, or equal, and recursively narrows the range. Binary Search has a time complexity of

O(log n), making it significantly faster than Linear Search. For instance, searching a sorted dataset of 1,000 items requires at most 10 comparisons.

Interpolation Search is a variant of Binary Search that assumes a uniform distribution of data. Instead of dividing the search space in half, it calculates the probable position of the target based on its value. This approach can achieve $O(\log \log n)$ performance in ideal cases but may degrade to $O(n)$ with skewed data distributions.

Exponential Search is useful for unbounded or infinite datasets. It starts by examining elements at exponentially increasing indices (e.g., 1, 2, 4, 8) until it finds a range containing the target. Once the range is identified, Binary Search is applied to locate the element. This hybrid approach combines the best of both methods, ensuring efficient performance.

Both sorting and searching techniques form the backbone of data processing in computer science, enabling efficient organization and retrieval of information in a variety of applications.

CHAPTER 9: NETWORKING AND COMMUNICATION

Basics of Computer Networks

A **computer network** is a collection of interconnected devices that communicate with each other to share resources, exchange information, and perform distributed tasks. These devices include computers, servers, routers, switches, and more. Understanding the basics of computer networks involves exploring how data is transmitted, the types of networks, and the protocols that govern communication.

At its core, a computer network relies on **data transmission**, which involves sending digital information in the form of binary signals (0s and 1s) across various mediums. These signals travel through physical media, such as copper wires, fiber optics, and wireless radio waves. Copper cables, like twisted pair or coaxial, are commonly used for short-distance communication, such as local area networks (LANs). Fiber optic cables, on the other hand, transmit data using light signals, enabling faster speeds and longer distances with minimal loss.

Wireless communication removes the need for physical cables, using technologies like Wi-Fi, Bluetooth, and cellular networks. Wi-Fi connects devices to local networks using radio signals within a limited range, while cellular networks enable wide-area connectivity through towers and satellites. These wireless technologies allow devices to connect seamlessly, even in remote locations.

Network topologies describe how devices in a network are arranged and connected. Common topologies include **star**, **bus**, **ring**, and **mesh**. In a star topology, all devices connect to a central hub or switch. If the hub fails, the entire network can be disrupted, but the failure of a single device doesn't affect others. A bus topology connects devices along a single cable, which makes it simple but prone to collisions and signal degradation as the number of devices increases. A ring topology connects devices in a circular loop, where data travels in one or both directions. This approach eliminates collisions but can be disrupted if a single link fails. Mesh topology offers redundancy by connecting devices to multiple others, ensuring data can take alternative routes in case of failures.

Network types are categorized based on their geographic coverage and purpose. A **local area network (LAN)** connects devices within a small area, such as an office or home. LANs use Ethernet cables or Wi-Fi for high-speed communication and are typically managed by a single organization. A **wide area network (WAN)**, like the internet, spans large distances and connects multiple LANs. WANs often use leased communication lines or satellite links to maintain connectivity. **Metropolitan area networks (MANs)**

are intermediate, covering cities or large campuses. **Personal area networks (PANs)** connect individual devices like smartphones, headphones, and wearables within a very short range using Bluetooth or similar technologies.

At the heart of any network are **network devices** that control data flow and connectivity. A **router** directs data packets between different networks, determining the best path for the data to travel. For example, a home router connects a LAN to the wider internet, translating private IP addresses into public ones using Network Address Translation (NAT). A **switch**, on the other hand, operates within a LAN, connecting devices and directing data based on their MAC addresses. Unlike hubs, which broadcast data to all devices, switches send data only to the intended recipient, reducing congestion and improving efficiency.

Communication in networks follows a structured model defined by **protocols**, which are rules for how data is transmitted and received. The **OSI (Open Systems Interconnection) model** organizes these protocols into seven layers: physical, data link, network, transport, session, presentation, and application. Each layer serves a specific function, ensuring seamless communication. For instance, the physical layer manages the transmission of raw bits over cables or wireless signals, while the transport layer ensures reliable delivery of data by managing retransmissions and error detection.

The **TCP/IP model** is a more practical and widely used alternative to the OSI model. It simplifies network communication into four layers: link, internet, transport, and application. The **internet layer** handles routing and addressing through the Internet Protocol (IP), assigning unique IP addresses to every device on the network. IPv4, with its 32-bit address space, supports approximately 4.3 billion unique addresses, but the growing number of devices has led to the adoption of **IPv6**, which uses 128-bit addresses to provide virtually unlimited addressing.

Data packets are the building blocks of network communication. When a device sends data, it is broken into smaller packets, each containing a portion of the data along with headers and metadata for routing. These packets travel independently across the network and are reassembled at the destination. For example, when you send an email, the message is split into packets that may take different routes through routers and switches before being reconstructed for the recipient.

MAC (Media Access Control) addresses are hardware-level identifiers assigned to network interfaces, ensuring that devices on the same network can communicate. MAC addresses are unique to each device and operate at the data link layer of the OSI model. While MAC addresses identify devices on a local network, **IP addresses** identify them globally, enabling communication across the internet.

DNS (Domain Name System) simplifies navigation on the internet by translating human-readable domain names, like www.example.com, into IP addresses. When you type a URL into your browser, your computer queries a DNS server to obtain the corresponding IP address, enabling it to connect to the correct server. This process is seamless, hiding the complexity of IP-based communication from the user.

Subnets divide larger networks into smaller, more manageable segments, improving performance and security. Each subnet operates as an isolated section of the network, with its own range of IP addresses. Subnetting reduces congestion by limiting broadcast traffic to devices within the same subnet and enhances security by isolating sensitive devices from the broader network.

Network security is an integral part of computer networks, protecting data from unauthorized access, theft, or damage. Firewalls, intrusion detection systems, and encryption protocols ensure that data remains secure during transmission. For instance, **SSL/TLS encryption** protects sensitive information, such as login credentials and payment details, by encrypting the data exchanged between your browser and a website.

Bandwidth and **latency** are critical metrics for evaluating network performance. Bandwidth measures the maximum amount of data that can be transmitted over a network in a given time, usually expressed in bits per second (bps). Higher bandwidth allows faster data transfer, improving user experience for activities like streaming or gaming. Latency, on the other hand, measures the delay between sending a request and receiving a response. Low latency is essential for real-time applications like video conferencing or online gaming, where even small delays can disrupt communication.

Wireless networks face additional challenges like **signal interference** and **range limitations**. Interference occurs when multiple devices use the same frequency band, such as the crowded 2.4 GHz band used by many Wi-Fi devices. Dual-band or tri-band routers mitigate this issue by offering additional channels in the 5 GHz band, which provides faster speeds over shorter distances.

Network scalability ensures that a network can accommodate growth, whether it's adding new devices, increasing traffic, or extending geographic coverage. Technologies like **VLANs (Virtual LANs)** and **SDN (Software-Defined Networking)** enhance scalability and flexibility. VLANs allow devices on separate physical networks to behave as though they are on the same LAN, while SDN centralizes network management, enabling administrators to dynamically configure and optimize network resources.

Cloud networking has transformed how organizations build and manage networks. By hosting infrastructure and services in the cloud, businesses reduce the need for on-premises hardware and gain access to scalable, on-demand resources. For example, virtual private networks (VPNs) create secure tunnels over the internet, connecting remote employees to corporate networks securely and efficiently.

From simple LANs to global WANs, computer networks form the backbone of modern communication and computing. They enable seamless data exchange, resource sharing, and collaboration across a diverse range of devices and technologies, shaping how we connect and interact in an increasingly digital world.

The OSI and TCP/IP Models

The **OSI (Open Systems Interconnection) model** and the **TCP/IP model** are conceptual frameworks that define how computer networks function. These models break down complex communication processes into layers, with each layer responsible for specific tasks. Understanding these layers helps developers and engineers design, troubleshoot, and optimize networks effectively.

The OSI model has **seven layers**, starting from the physical layer at the bottom and ending with the application layer at the top. Each layer interacts with the one above and below it, ensuring seamless data flow from one device to another.

1. **Physical Layer**: This layer handles the transmission of raw bits over a communication medium, such as cables, fiber optics, or wireless signals. It includes specifications for voltage levels, data rates, and physical connectors. For example, Ethernet cables and Wi-Fi signals operate at this layer.

2. **Data Link Layer**: The data link layer manages error detection, correction, and framing. It ensures reliable data transfer between two nodes on the same network. Protocols like Ethernet and Wi-Fi work here, using **MAC addresses** to identify devices.

3. **Network Layer**: This layer handles routing and addressing, ensuring that data packets travel from the source to the destination across multiple networks. The **Internet Protocol (IP)** operates at this layer, providing logical addressing (e.g., IPv4 or IPv6).

4. **Transport Layer**: The transport layer provides reliable data delivery, including segmentation, error recovery, and flow control. **TCP (Transmission Control Protocol)** ensures ordered and reliable delivery, while **UDP (User Datagram Protocol)** offers faster but less reliable communication.

5. **Session Layer**: This layer establishes, manages, and terminates communication sessions between devices. It ensures that data streams are synchronized and maintained across devices.

6. **Presentation Layer**: The presentation layer translates data into a format that the application layer can understand. It handles encryption, compression, and data translation. For instance, converting JPEG image files into displayable pixels happens here.

7. **Application Layer**: At the top of the OSI model, the application layer provides services directly to the user. Protocols like HTTP, FTP, and SMTP enable web browsing, file transfers, and email communication.

The **TCP/IP model** is more streamlined, with only **four layers**: link, internet, transport, and application. It simplifies the OSI model by combining some of its layers and aligning closely with real-world implementations.

1. **Link Layer**: This is equivalent to the OSI physical and data link layers, managing hardware-level communication and local network protocols.

2. **Internet Layer**: Corresponding to the OSI network layer, it ensures packet delivery across networks using IP. Routing and addressing are key functions of this layer.

3. **Transport Layer**: The TCP/IP transport layer maps directly to the OSI transport layer, handling reliable delivery through TCP or faster, connectionless delivery with UDP.

4. **Application Layer**: This combines the OSI session, presentation, and application layers into a single layer. Protocols like HTTP, DNS, and SMTP operate here.

While the OSI model is often used as a theoretical framework, the TCP/IP model reflects how networks actually function. For instance, the internet relies heavily on TCP/IP protocols for communication between devices worldwide. Both models help network professionals understand the flow of data, troubleshoot issues, and implement security measures effectively.

Network Security Fundamentals

Network security is essential for protecting data, devices, and systems from unauthorized access, theft, and damage. As networks grow in complexity and importance, the risks they face also increase. Security measures encompass a combination of technologies, protocols, and practices to safeguard communication and ensure system integrity.

Firewalls are the first line of defense in network security, acting as barriers between trusted internal networks and untrusted external networks. Firewalls monitor and control incoming and outgoing traffic based on predefined rules. For example, a firewall might block traffic from suspicious IP addresses or restrict access to specific ports. Firewalls can be implemented as hardware appliances, software applications, or a combination of both.

Encryption ensures that data remains secure during transmission by converting it into a format that unauthorized users cannot read. **SSL (Secure Sockets Layer)** and **TLS (Transport Layer Security)** are widely used encryption protocols that protect web traffic. When you visit a secure website, the HTTPS protocol encrypts the data exchanged between your browser and the server, preventing eavesdropping and tampering.

Virtual Private Networks (VPNs) provide secure communication over public networks by creating encrypted tunnels between devices. For example, a remote employee can use a VPN to securely access a company's internal network from home. VPNs use protocols like **IPSec** and **OpenVPN** to protect data from interception and ensure privacy.

Authentication mechanisms verify the identity of users and devices before granting access to a network. Passwords are the simplest form of authentication, but they are often combined with additional measures for enhanced security. **Two-factor authentication (2FA)** requires users to provide two forms of verification, such as a password and a code sent to their phone. **Biometric authentication** uses physical traits like fingerprints or facial recognition, offering a higher level of security.

Access control ensures that users and devices can only access resources they are authorized to use. **Role-Based Access Control (RBAC)** assigns permissions based on roles within an organization, limiting access to sensitive data. For example, a finance department employee might have access to payroll systems but not engineering project files.

Intrusion detection and prevention systems (IDS/IPS) monitor network traffic for suspicious activity. An IDS alerts administrators when it detects potential threats, while an IPS takes proactive measures to block malicious traffic. These systems analyze data patterns, looking for signs of attacks such as unusual login attempts or traffic spikes.

Network segmentation divides a network into smaller sections, limiting the spread of attacks. For instance, separating a guest Wi-Fi network from the internal corporate network ensures that compromised guest devices cannot access sensitive company data. **VLANs (Virtual Local Area Networks)** are commonly used for segmentation, creating isolated environments within a single physical network.

Endpoint security focuses on protecting individual devices, such as laptops, smartphones, and IoT devices, which often serve as entry points for attackers. Antivirus software, firewalls, and patch management are critical components of endpoint security. Regular updates and patches address vulnerabilities in operating systems and applications, reducing the risk of exploitation.

DDoS (Distributed Denial of Service) attacks are a common threat to network security. These attacks flood a target server or network with massive amounts of traffic, overwhelming its resources and causing service disruptions. Mitigating DDoS attacks requires specialized tools like traffic filtering, rate limiting, and cloud-based protection services.

Phishing is another significant threat, where attackers trick users into revealing sensitive information through fake emails, websites, or messages. Training users to recognize phishing attempts and deploying email filters are effective countermeasures. Multi-factor authentication can also reduce the impact of compromised credentials.

Zero Trust Architecture (ZTA) is an emerging approach to network security that assumes no device or user is trustworthy by default. ZTA requires continuous verification of identity and context for every access request, regardless of whether it originates inside or outside the network perimeter. This model reduces the risk of lateral movement by attackers who gain initial access.

Security monitoring is an ongoing process that involves analyzing network traffic, logs, and alerts to detect and respond to threats. Tools like **SIEM (Security Information and Event Management)** systems aggregate and analyze data from multiple sources, providing insights into potential vulnerabilities and incidents.

Network security also involves **physical security measures**, such as securing server rooms, limiting access to network hardware, and using locks or biometric scanners. Without physical protection, attackers could bypass digital defenses by tampering with hardware.

As threats evolve, **penetration testing** and **red teaming** help organizations identify weaknesses in their defenses. Penetration testing simulates attacks to uncover vulnerabilities, while red teams act as adversaries to test the effectiveness of security measures in real-world scenarios.

Wireless Communication Protocols

Wireless communication protocols enable devices to connect and communicate without physical cables, leveraging radio waves, infrared, or other wireless technologies.

These protocols provide the foundation for modern connectivity, supporting everything from mobile phones to IoT devices and high-speed internet.

One of the most widely used wireless communication protocols is **Wi-Fi (Wireless Fidelity)**, based on the IEEE 802.11 family of standards. Wi-Fi allows devices like laptops, smartphones, and smart home gadgets to connect to local area networks (LANs) without physical wiring. The technology operates in two main frequency bands: **2.4 GHz** and **5 GHz**, with newer Wi-Fi 6 (802.11ax) adding support for the **6 GHz band**. The 2.4 GHz band provides broader coverage but slower speeds, while the 5 GHz and 6 GHz bands offer faster speeds with reduced range. Wi-Fi uses encryption protocols like **WPA2** and **WPA3** to secure communications, ensuring that data exchanged over the network remains private.

Another ubiquitous protocol is **Bluetooth**, which facilitates short-range communication between devices like headphones, keyboards, and smartwatches. Unlike Wi-Fi, Bluetooth is designed for low-power operation, making it ideal for battery-powered devices. **Bluetooth Low Energy (BLE)**, introduced in Bluetooth 4.0, further optimizes energy consumption for applications like fitness trackers and IoT sensors. BLE achieves this by transmitting data in short bursts, maintaining low power usage while ensuring reliable communication.

Zigbee is another protocol tailored for low-power, low-data-rate applications, commonly used in smart home systems and industrial automation. Zigbee operates in the **2.4 GHz ISM band**, enabling devices to form **mesh networks** where data can hop between devices to reach its destination. This mesh capability enhances coverage and reliability, especially in environments with obstacles or interference. Zigbee's low power requirements make it suitable for devices like smart light bulbs and temperature sensors that need to operate for years on a single battery.

Z-Wave, similar to Zigbee, is a wireless protocol designed for smart home devices. Operating in the sub-1 GHz frequency band, Z-Wave avoids the interference issues often encountered with 2.4 GHz protocols. Its design emphasizes interoperability, ensuring that Z-Wave devices from different manufacturers can work seamlessly together. Z-Wave also uses mesh networking to extend range and improve reliability, making it a popular choice for home automation hubs and security systems.

For long-range wireless communication, **LoRa (Long Range)** and **LoRaWAN (LoRa Wide Area Network)** are standout protocols. LoRa operates in unlicensed frequency bands and is optimized for low-power, wide-area network (LPWAN) applications like smart agriculture, environmental monitoring, and utility metering. LoRaWAN adds a network layer to LoRa, enabling centralized management and bi-directional communication between devices and gateways. Its range can extend up to 15 kilometers in rural areas, making it ideal for connecting sensors and devices spread over large distances.

Cellular communication protocols, such as **4G LTE (Long Term Evolution)** and **5G**, provide the backbone for mobile networks. LTE enables high-speed internet, voice calls, and messaging, supporting applications like video streaming and online gaming. **5G** builds on LTE with improved speed, lower latency, and the capacity to handle millions of connected devices simultaneously. This capability makes 5G critical for future technologies like autonomous vehicles and smart cities. Cellular networks operate on licensed frequency bands, ensuring minimal interference and reliable performance.

NFC (Near Field Communication) is a short-range protocol that facilitates secure, contactless communication between devices. NFC operates at a range of about 4 centimeters and is commonly used for mobile payments, access control, and device pairing. For example, tapping a smartphone against a payment terminal initiates an encrypted transaction, leveraging NFC's simplicity and security.

Infrared (IR) is another wireless protocol, often used in remote controls for TVs and other consumer electronics. Unlike radio-frequency protocols, IR relies on line-of-sight communication, meaning that devices must be aligned without obstacles blocking the signal. While less versatile than Wi-Fi or Bluetooth, IR remains a reliable solution for basic, short-range communication.

In the realm of **industrial applications**, **WirelessHART** and **ISA100.11a** are protocols designed for wireless sensor networks in manufacturing and process industries. These protocols operate in the 2.4 GHz band and provide robust communication in environments with significant interference, such as factories. WirelessHART uses **time-synchronized, self-healing mesh networking**, ensuring that data continues to flow even if some nodes fail or encounter interference.

Thread is a relatively new wireless protocol, designed specifically for IoT applications. It provides low-latency, secure communication between devices and supports IPv6, enabling seamless integration with the internet. Thread operates in the 2.4 GHz band and uses mesh networking to ensure reliable communication in smart homes and buildings.

For high-speed wireless data transfer over short distances, **Ultra-Wideband (UWB)** is gaining traction. UWB uses a wide spectrum of frequencies and very low power to achieve precise location tracking and high-speed communication. Applications for UWB include indoor positioning systems, secure keyless entry for vehicles, and advanced AR/ VR systems.

WiMAX (Worldwide Interoperability for Microwave Access) is a protocol designed for long-range, high-speed wireless broadband. Often compared to Wi-Fi, WiMAX operates over larger areas, providing connectivity to rural or underserved regions. It uses licensed frequency bands and supports applications like backhaul connections for mobile networks and fixed wireless internet.

Wireless protocols for vehicular communication, such as **DSRC (Dedicated Short-Range Communications)** and **C-V2X (Cellular Vehicle-to-Everything)**, enable vehicles to communicate with each other and with infrastructure. These protocols support applications like collision avoidance, traffic management, and autonomous driving. DSRC operates in the 5.9 GHz band and focuses on low-latency communication, while C-V2X leverages cellular networks to provide broader coverage and advanced capabilities.

The proliferation of wireless protocols addresses the diverse needs of modern communication, from short-range device pairing to wide-area connectivity. Each protocol is designed with specific trade-offs in mind, balancing factors like speed, range, power consumption, and reliability. As technology advances, these protocols continue to evolve, enabling new applications and driving innovation across industries.

CHAPTER 10: DATABASES AND DATA MANAGEMENT

Types of Databases: Relational vs. NoSQL

Databases are essential for storing, managing, and retrieving data efficiently. They come in various types, but the two most commonly used are **relational databases** and **NoSQL databases**. Each has its strengths, limitations, and ideal use cases, depending on the requirements of the application.

Relational databases (RDBMS) organize data into tables, where each table represents a specific entity, such as customers, orders, or products. The rows in a table are called **records**, and each record is an instance of the entity, while the columns are **attributes** or fields representing the properties of the entity. For example, a table named `Customers` might have columns for `CustomerID`, `Name`, and `Email`, with each row representing a single customer.

The defining feature of relational databases is their reliance on **Structured Query Language (SQL)** for data manipulation and querying. SQL provides powerful commands like `SELECT`, `INSERT`, `UPDATE`, and `DELETE`, enabling users to interact with the data easily. A query like `SELECT * FROM Customers WHERE Name = 'Alice';` retrieves all records where the name is "Alice". SQL's consistency and standardization make relational databases a popular choice across industries.

Relational databases are based on the principles of **normalization**, which minimizes redundancy and organizes data into smaller, interrelated tables. Relationships between these tables are established using **primary keys** and **foreign keys**. A primary key is a unique identifier for each record in a table, while a foreign key links a record in one table to a related record in another. For instance, an `Orders` table might have a foreign key referencing the `CustomerID` in the `Customers` table, linking each order to a specific customer. This structure ensures data integrity and eliminates inconsistencies.

One of the key advantages of relational databases is their adherence to **ACID (Atomicity, Consistency, Isolation, Durability)** properties, which ensure reliable transactions. Atomicity guarantees that a transaction is treated as a single unit, meaning either all operations within it succeed, or none are applied. Consistency ensures the database remains in a valid state after a transaction. Isolation prevents concurrent transactions from interfering with each other, and durability ensures that committed transactions are permanently saved, even in the event of a system failure.

Popular relational database management systems include **MySQL**, **PostgreSQL**, **Oracle Database**, and **Microsoft SQL Server**. These systems are widely used in applications where structured data and transactional integrity are critical, such as banking, e-commerce, and enterprise resource planning (ERP) systems.

Despite their strengths, relational databases have limitations. They struggle with handling **unstructured or semi-structured data**, such as JSON documents, images, or videos. Scaling relational databases horizontally — distributing data across multiple servers — is challenging due to their rigid schema and interdependent tables. These limitations have driven the adoption of **NoSQL databases** for modern applications requiring greater flexibility and scalability.

NoSQL databases are designed to handle large volumes of unstructured, semi-structured, or rapidly changing data. Unlike relational databases, NoSQL systems do not rely on fixed schemas, allowing developers to store data in formats that best suit their applications. This flexibility is particularly useful for agile development environments, where requirements evolve over time.

NoSQL databases are categorized into several types, each optimized for specific data models and use cases. **Document databases** store data as documents, typically in JSON or BSON format. Each document contains fields and values, much like a record in a relational database, but without a rigid structure. For example, in a document database like **MongoDB**, a customer record might include fields for `Name`, `Email`, and `Address`, while another record might omit the `Address` field or include additional fields like `PhoneNumber`. This flexibility allows applications to evolve without requiring schema migrations.

Key-value stores are another type of NoSQL database, where data is stored as key-value pairs. The key serves as a unique identifier, and the value can be any type of data, from simple text to complex objects. Key-value stores like **Redis** and **Amazon DynamoDB** are highly performant and are often used for caching, session management, and real-time analytics. For instance, a key-value store might store a user session with the key as the session ID and the value as the user's session data.

Column-family stores, such as **Apache Cassandra** and **HBase**, organize data into rows and columns but allow flexible column definitions. Each row can have a variable number of columns, grouped into families. These databases are well-suited for handling time-series data, logs, or other applications requiring high write throughput and scalable storage.

Graph databases like **Neo4j** and **Amazon Neptune** specialize in representing and querying data with complex relationships. Instead of tables, they use nodes, edges, and properties to model entities and their connections. For example, a social network application might use a graph database to represent users as nodes and their friendships as edges, making it easy to query relationships like "Who are Alice's friends of friends?"

NoSQL databases often prioritize **BASE (Basically Available, Soft state, Eventually consistent)** properties over ACID guarantees. This trade-off allows them to scale horizontally, handling massive amounts of data across distributed systems. Horizontal scaling is achieved by **sharding**, where data is divided across multiple servers. For example, an e-commerce site might shard its product catalog across several servers, enabling faster access and reducing bottlenecks during peak traffic.

One limitation of NoSQL databases is their lack of robust consistency guarantees. While eventual consistency is acceptable for applications like social media feeds, it may not be suitable for critical systems like financial transactions. Additionally, the lack of a standardized query language like SQL means developers must learn the specific APIs and query mechanisms for each NoSQL database.

Relational and NoSQL databases often complement each other in modern architectures. For example, a relational database might handle transactional data, such as orders and payments, while a NoSQL database stores unstructured data, like user-generated content or product recommendations. This hybrid approach leverages the strengths of both types of databases.

When choosing between relational and NoSQL databases, factors like data structure, scalability needs, and consistency requirements should guide the decision. Relational databases excel in structured, transaction-heavy environments, while NoSQL databases are ideal for flexible, high-scale applications.

Database Design and Normalization

Database design is the process of structuring a database to efficiently store, manage, and retrieve data while minimizing redundancy and ensuring consistency. A well-designed database supports the needs of an application, ensuring scalability, performance, and reliability. The process involves understanding the requirements, identifying the entities and relationships, and creating a schema that reflects the data model.

The first step in database design is identifying the **entities**—real-world objects or concepts that need to be represented in the database. For example, in an e-commerce application, entities might include `Customers`, `Products`, `Orders`, and `Payments`. Each entity is represented as a table, with **attributes** as columns. For instance, the `Customers` table might have attributes like `CustomerID`, `Name`, `Email`, and `Address`.

Once the entities and attributes are identified, relationships between them are defined. **One-to-one (1:1)** relationships are rare and usually represent tightly related entities. For example, a `User` table might have a one-to-one relationship with a `Profile` table.

One-to-many (1:N) relationships are more common, such as a `Customer` having multiple `Orders`. In this case, a foreign key in the `Orders` table references the primary key in the `Customers` table. **Many-to-many (M:N)** relationships, like `Students` enrolling in `Courses`, require an intermediate table, often called a **junction table**, to manage the relationship.

To maintain data integrity and reduce redundancy, database design employs **normalization**, a process that organizes tables into smaller, related structures. **First Normal Form (1NF)** requires that tables have no repeating groups and that each column contains atomic values. For example, a `Products` table should not have columns like `Color1`, `Color2`, and `Color3` for different product colors. Instead, it should store each color in a separate row.

Second Normal Form (2NF) eliminates partial dependencies, where a non-key attribute depends only on part of a composite primary key. For instance, if a table storing `OrderDetails` uses a composite primary key of `OrderID` and `ProductID`, any attribute like `ProductName` that depends only on `ProductID` should be moved to a separate `Products` table.

Third Normal Form (3NF) eliminates transitive dependencies, where non-key attributes depend on other non-key attributes. For example, if a `Customers` table includes `City` and `ZipCode`, and `City` can be derived from `ZipCode`, `City` should be moved to a separate `Locations` table.

While normalization improves consistency and reduces redundancy, it can lead to **performance trade-offs** in read-heavy systems, as queries may need to join multiple tables. In such cases, **denormalization** is used strategically to improve performance by duplicating certain data. For instance, storing a customer's name directly in an `Orders` table can eliminate the need for a join when querying order details.

Indexes are another critical aspect of database design, improving query performance by enabling faster lookups. **Primary indexes** are automatically created for primary keys, while additional **secondary indexes** can be added to frequently queried columns. For example, indexing the `Email` column in a `Customers` table allows efficient searches for specific customers by email. However, excessive indexing can increase write overhead and storage requirements, so indexes must be used judiciously.

Database design also incorporates constraints to ensure data integrity. **Unique constraints** prevent duplicate entries in a column, such as ensuring that each email in a `Users` table is unique. **Check constraints** enforce specific conditions, like requiring that an `OrderAmount` be greater than zero. **Foreign key constraints** maintain referential integrity by ensuring that referenced keys in related tables exist.

Designing for scalability is another key consideration. Horizontal scaling, or **sharding**, involves splitting large tables across multiple servers based on criteria like geographic region or user ID. Vertical scaling focuses on optimizing server performance, such as upgrading hardware or using in-memory databases for faster processing.

Querying with SQL

SQL (Structured Query Language) is the standard language for interacting with relational databases, allowing users to retrieve/manipulate/manage data using concise/intuitive commands. SQL is essential for database admins, developers, and analysts.

The **SELECT statement** is the cornerstone of SQL, used to retrieve data from one or more tables. A basic query like `SELECT * FROM Customers;` fetches all columns and rows from the `Customers` table. To retrieve specific columns, you can specify them explicitly, such as `SELECT Name, Email FROM Customers;`. Adding a **WHERE clause** filters rows based on conditions, like `SELECT * FROM Orders WHERE OrderDate > '2025-01-01';`, which retrieves orders placed after January 1, 2025.

SQL supports **aggregate functions** to perform calculations on data, such as counting rows, summing values, or finding averages. For instance, `SELECT COUNT(*) FROM Orders WHERE Status = 'Completed';` returns the total number of completed orders. Other common functions include `SUM`, `AVG`, `MAX`, and `MIN`. These functions are often combined with **GROUP BY** to organize results by categories. For example, `SELECT CustomerID, SUM(TotalAmount) FROM Orders GROUP BY CustomerID;` calculates the total order amount for each customer.

Joining tables is a powerful feature of SQL, allowing you to combine data from related tables. A **INNER JOIN** retrieves rows that have matching values in both tables. For example, `SELECT Customers.Name, Orders.OrderDate FROM Customers INNER JOIN Orders ON Customers.CustomerID = Orders.CustomerID;` combines customer names with their order dates. **LEFT JOINs** include all rows from the left table and matching rows from the right table, while **RIGHT JOINs** do the opposite. **FULL OUTER JOINs** include all rows from both tables, with NULLs for non-matching rows.

SQL also supports **subqueries**, which are queries nested within another query. Subqueries are useful for complex operations, like finding customers who placed orders above a certain amount:

```
SELECT Name FROM Customers WHERE CustomerID IN (SELECT
CustomerID FROM Orders WHERE TotalAmount > 500);
```

In addition to querying data, SQL allows for **data manipulation** with commands like `INSERT`, `UPDATE`, and `DELETE`. To add a new record to a table, use `INSERT INTO`, such as:

```
INSERT INTO Products (ProductName, Price) VALUES ('Laptop',
1200);.
```

Updating existing records involves the `UPDATE` command, for example:
```
UPDATE Orders SET Status = 'Shipped' WHERE OrderID = 102;.
```
To remove records, use `DELETE`, such as:

```
DELETE FROM Customers WHERE LastLogin < '2024-01-01';.
```

SQL also includes **transaction control commands** like `BEGIN`, `COMMIT`, and `ROLLBACK`. Transactions group multiple operations into a single unit of work, ensuring atomicity. For example, transferring money between accounts involves debiting one account and crediting another. A transaction ensures both actions succeed or neither occurs:

```
BEGIN; UPDATE Accounts SET Balance = Balance - 500 WHERE
AccountID = 1; UPDATE Accounts SET Balance = Balance + 500
WHERE AccountID = 2; COMMIT;.
```

To enhance query performance, SQL allows the use of **indexes**. For example, creating an index on the `OrderDate` column of the `Orders` table speeds up queries filtering by date:

```
CREATE INDEX idx_order_date ON Orders (OrderDate);.
```

However, indexes increase storage requirements and slow down write operations, so they must be applied strategically.

SQL also provides **user-defined functions (UDFs)** and **stored procedures** for reusable logic. A UDF might calculate tax rates, while a stored procedure performs a series of operations like processing payroll. For example, a stored procedure to update inventory after an order might look like:

```
CREATE PROCEDURE UpdateInventory (OrderID INT) BEGIN UPDATE
Inventory SET Quantity = Quantity - (SELECT Quantity FROM
OrderDetails WHERE OrderDetails.OrderID = OrderID); END;.
```

CHAPTER 11: SOFTWARE ENGINEERING PRINCIPLES

Software Development Life Cycle (SDLC)

The **Software Development Life Cycle (SDLC)** is a structured approach to developing software, ensuring projects are completed efficiently and meet user requirements. It divides the software creation process into distinct phases, each with specific goals, deliverables, and review points. This framework helps teams manage complexity, reduce errors, and maintain quality throughout development.

The **first phase** of the SDLC is **Requirement Analysis**. In this phase, stakeholders, including clients, users, and developers, work together to define what the software should do. Teams gather functional requirements, such as what features the system will include, and non-functional requirements, such as performance, scalability, and security constraints. Business analysts often create detailed documentation, like a Software Requirements Specification (SRS), which acts as a contract between stakeholders and developers. Clear, well-documented requirements are critical because they form the foundation for all subsequent phases.

Once requirements are defined, the process moves to the **System Design** phase. Here, architects and developers plan how the software will achieve the specified requirements. They create high-level designs that outline the system's structure, including architecture diagrams, data flow diagrams, and database schemas. For example, a web application might adopt a three-tier architecture with a front-end user interface, a middle-tier application server, and a back-end database. Detailed designs may include algorithms, user interface mockups, and API specifications. This phase ensures that everyone agrees on how the system will be built before actual development begins.

The **Implementation** phase is where developers write code based on the designs. This phase involves selecting appropriate programming languages, frameworks, and tools to build the software. For example, a mobile app might use Swift for iOS or Kotlin for Android, while a web application might use JavaScript frameworks like React or Angular. Developers often break the work into smaller tasks or modules, enabling parallel development. Version control systems, such as Git, are used to manage code changes and facilitate collaboration among team members. Writing clean, well-documented code is essential, as it affects maintainability and future updates.

Once the software is built, it enters the **Testing** phase. Quality assurance (QA) engineers verify that the software meets the requirements and is free of defects. Testing includes several levels: **unit testing**, where individual components are tested in isolation; **integration testing**, which ensures that components work together; **system testing**, which evaluates the entire application; and **acceptance testing**, where users validate that the software meets their needs. Automated testing tools, like Selenium or JUnit, are often used to speed up the process and ensure consistency. Bugs found during this phase are reported, fixed, and retested until the software is deemed stable.

The next phase is **Deployment**, where the software is released to its intended environment, such as production servers or app stores. Deployment strategies vary depending on the application and its users. **Big Bang deployment** involves releasing the entire system at once, suitable for smaller applications or updates. **Phased deployment** introduces features incrementally, minimizing risks by testing changes with a subset of users before a full rollout. **Blue-Green deployment** maintains two identical environments: one active (blue) and one idle (green). New updates are deployed to the idle environment and, once validated, traffic is switched to it, ensuring zero downtime.

Following deployment, the software enters the **Maintenance** phase. In this phase, developers address issues reported by users, implement new features, and adapt the system to changing requirements. Maintenance can be categorized into three types: **corrective maintenance**, which fixes bugs and defects; **adaptive maintenance**, which modifies the software to accommodate environmental changes, like new operating systems or browsers; and **perfective maintenance**, which enhances functionality or performance based on user feedback. Effective maintenance ensures the software remains relevant and useful over time.

The SDLC also emphasizes iterative development through models like **Agile** and **DevOps**, which have become popular alternatives to traditional, linear approaches like the **Waterfall model**. Agile divides the project into small, manageable increments called **sprints**, each lasting 1-4 weeks. At the end of each sprint, a functional portion of the software is delivered, enabling teams to adapt to changing requirements. DevOps, on the other hand, integrates development and operations, automating processes like testing and deployment to accelerate delivery and improve reliability.

Metrics and tools are used throughout the SDLC to monitor progress and quality. For example, **burndown charts** track remaining work in Agile projects, while **static code analysis tools**, like SonarQube, identify potential issues in code before testing. These tools help teams identify bottlenecks, measure productivity, and ensure adherence to best practices.

Communication is a critical aspect of the SDLC. Regular meetings, such as **daily stand-ups**, sprint reviews, and retrospectives, keep team members aligned and focused. Stakeholder involvement at key milestones ensures that the project remains on track and meets expectations. Documentation, including technical specifications, user manuals, and maintenance guides, provides a record of decisions and facilitates knowledge transfer.

Version Control Systems

Version control systems (VCS) are tools that track changes to code, documents, and other files over time. They enable developers to collaborate efficiently, maintain a history of modifications, and revert to earlier versions when necessary. These systems are essential for modern software development, where teams often work on the same codebase across different locations.

At the core of a VCS is the concept of **repositories**, which store the files and their change history. A repository can be local, residing on a developer's machine, or remote, hosted on a server accessible by multiple contributors. Developers use commands like `commit` to save changes to the repository, recording a snapshot of the current state of the files. Each commit includes a **unique identifier (hash)** and a message describing the changes, providing a clear history of modifications.

VCS tools are divided into two main types: **centralized** and **distributed**. In a **centralized version control system (CVCS)**, such as **Subversion (SVN)** or **Perforce**, a single central repository stores all the data. Developers pull files from the central server to their local machines and commit changes back to it. While centralized systems are simple and effective for smaller teams, they rely heavily on the server's availability. If the central server goes down, developers lose access to the repository.

Distributed version control systems (DVCS), like **Git** and **Mercurial**, offer greater flexibility by giving each developer a complete copy of the repository, including the full history. Changes can be committed locally without requiring an internet connection, and updates can later be synchronized with a remote repository. This decentralized model allows for **branching and merging**, enabling developers to work on different features or fixes simultaneously without interfering with each other's work.

Branching is a powerful feature in version control, allowing developers to create separate lines of development. For example, a team might use a `main` branch for stable releases, a `develop` branch for ongoing work, and feature branches for specific enhancements. Once a feature is complete, it can be merged back into the `develop` branch. Tools like Git simplify this process, offering commands like `git branch` to create branches and `git merge` to combine them. **Pull requests** (or merge requests) are used in collaborative workflows to review changes before integrating them into the main codebase.

Version control also facilitates **conflict resolution**, which occurs when multiple developers modify the same file simultaneously. The VCS highlights conflicting changes and allows developers to resolve them manually. For example, if two developers edit different parts of a function in the same file, the system merges their changes automatically. However, if they alter the same lines, the VCS marks a conflict and requires intervention.

Remote repositories are often hosted on platforms like **GitHub**, **GitLab**, or **Bitbucket**, which provide additional tools for collaboration and project management. These platforms offer features like issue tracking, wikis, and CI/CD pipelines, integrating seamlessly with the version control workflow. For instance, GitHub Actions allows teams to automate tasks like running tests or deploying code when changes are pushed to a repository.

Version control systems also enable **rollback and recovery**, allowing developers to undo changes or revert to a previous version of the codebase. Commands like `git revert` or `git reset` in Git provide flexibility for handling mistakes. For example, if a recent commit introduces a bug, the team can easily restore the code to its previous state without losing unrelated updates.

Tagging is another useful feature of VCS, enabling developers to mark specific commits as milestones, such as **releases** or **hotfixes**. Tags like `v1.0` or `v2.1` help identify stable versions of the software, making it easier to reference or deploy them later.

Testing and Debugging Techniques

Testing and debugging are essential practices in software development that ensure the reliability and functionality of applications. While testing focuses on identifying issues before software is deployed, debugging involves diagnosing and fixing those issues in the code.

Testing begins with **unit testing**, where individual components or functions are tested in isolation to ensure they behave as expected. Unit tests often use frameworks like **JUnit** for Java, **PyTest** for Python, or **Mocha** for JavaScript. These tests verify the correctness of small pieces of code, such as a function calculating a discount or formatting a date. Writing unit tests alongside code development promotes a **test-driven development (TDD)** approach, where developers create tests before implementing the actual functionality.

Integration testing follows unit testing and focuses on verifying how different components of the software work together. For example, in a web application, integration tests might check the interaction between the front-end UI and the back-end API. These tests ensure that data flows correctly between systems and that dependencies are functioning as intended.

System testing evaluates the entire application as a whole. This level of testing checks whether the software meets the defined requirements and works as expected in its target environment. System tests often simulate real-world scenarios, such as a user logging in, performing a search, and making a purchase. Tools like **Selenium** are commonly used for automated system testing in web applications.

Acceptance testing is the final phase of testing before deployment, performed to validate that the software meets the needs of its users. This testing is often conducted by end-users or stakeholders and includes verifying functionality, usability, and performance under realistic conditions. If the software passes acceptance testing, it is deemed ready for release.

Automated testing is a critical technique for improving efficiency and consistency, especially in large projects with frequent updates. Scripts and tools execute predefined test cases automatically, reducing the time and effort required for manual testing. For example, continuous integration pipelines often include automated tests that run whenever new code is committed, ensuring that changes don't introduce regressions.

When bugs are discovered during testing, debugging begins. Debugging starts with **reproducing the issue** to understand its behavior and scope. Developers often use logging or breakpoints to inspect the program's state at different points during execution. For example, if a function returns an incorrect value, placing a breakpoint inside the function allows the developer to step through the code and identify where the logic deviates.

Debugging tools, such as **IDE debuggers** or standalone tools like **GDB**, provide features like variable inspection, stack tracing, and conditional breakpoints. These tools make it easier to isolate and resolve problems. For instance, a stack trace reveals the sequence of function calls leading to an error, helping developers pinpoint the source of the issue.

A common debugging technique is **binary search debugging**, which involves narrowing down the source of the problem by systematically eliminating sections of code. For example, if a bug affects the output of a report, the developer might disable half the code generating the report to determine whether the issue persists. Repeating this process helps isolate the faulty section.

Regression testing ensures that recent changes or fixes do not introduce new bugs in existing functionality. Automated regression test suites are often run after every significant update to verify that previously tested features remain stable.

For complex systems, **stress testing** and **load testing** evaluate how the application performs under heavy usage. Stress testing involves pushing the system to its limits, such as simulating thousands of concurrent users, to identify bottlenecks or failure points.

Load testing measures performance under expected levels of traffic, ensuring the system can handle its intended workload efficiently.

Pair debugging, where two developers collaborate to solve an issue, is another effective technique. One developer explains the code and issue aloud, while the other provides insights or suggestions. This collaborative approach often uncovers problems more quickly than debugging alone.

Debugging is iterative, requiring persistence and creativity to address the unexpected. Effective testing and debugging not only improve software quality but also foster confidence among developers and users, ensuring that the final product meets expectations.

Agile Methodologies

Agile methodologies are a set of principles and practices designed to promote flexibility, collaboration, and iterative progress in software development. Agile moves away from rigid, linear development processes like the Waterfall model, focusing instead on delivering smaller, incremental improvements that add value quickly while accommodating changes throughout the project.

At the heart of Agile is the **Agile Manifesto**, which emphasizes individuals and interactions over processes and tools, working software over comprehensive documentation, customer collaboration over contract negotiation, and responding to change over following a plan. These principles guide teams to adapt their workflows to prioritize value and efficiency.

One of the most widely used Agile frameworks is **Scrum**, which organizes work into time-boxed iterations called **sprints**, typically lasting 1 to 4 weeks. Each sprint begins with a **sprint planning meeting**, where the team selects tasks from the **product backlog**, a prioritized list of features, bugs, and improvements maintained by the **product owner**. These tasks are added to the **sprint backlog**, forming the team's workload for the sprint. The team commits to delivering these items by the end of the sprint.

Daily **stand-up meetings** are a hallmark of Scrum, fostering transparency and communication. During these brief meetings, each team member answers three questions: What did I accomplish yesterday? What will I work on today? Are there any blockers impeding my progress? These updates help the team stay aligned and identify issues early, preventing delays.

At the end of the sprint, the team demonstrates the completed work during the **sprint review**, gathering feedback from stakeholders. This feedback is incorporated into the product backlog, ensuring that future sprints address the evolving needs of the users and business. Following the review, the team conducts a **sprint retrospective** to reflect on the sprint's successes and challenges, identifying ways to improve their process for the next iteration.

Another popular Agile framework is **Kanban**, which emphasizes continuous delivery and visual workflow management. Kanban boards display tasks in columns, such as "To Do," "In Progress," and "Done," providing a clear view of the team's work at any given time. Teams limit the number of tasks in each column, known as **work-in-progress (WIP) limits,** to prevent bottlenecks and maintain a steady flow of work. For example, if the "In Progress" column is full, no new tasks can be started until some are completed. This focus on flow helps teams deliver work incrementally and avoid overloading team members.

Extreme Programming (XP) is another Agile methodology, known for its focus on technical practices and delivering high-quality code. XP encourages practices like **pair programming,** where two developers work together on the same code, with one writing and the other reviewing. This collaboration improves code quality and fosters knowledge sharing. XP also emphasizes **test-driven development (TDD)**, where developers write automated tests before implementing the corresponding functionality. This approach ensures that code meets requirements and reduces the likelihood of bugs.

XP also advocates for frequent releases and continuous feedback, promoting **refactoring** to improve the codebase without changing its behavior. Refactoring ensures that the software remains maintainable and scalable as new features are added. For example, simplifying a complex algorithm or reorganizing code into smaller, reusable functions makes it easier to update and debug.

Lean Software Development, another Agile approach, focuses on eliminating waste and maximizing value delivery. Waste can take many forms, such as unnecessary features, delays, or inefficient processes. Lean encourages teams to prioritize work that directly contributes to user satisfaction and business goals. Practices like **just-in-time delivery**, where tasks are started only when needed, and **building quality in**, where testing is integrated into every stage of development, align with this philosophy.

Collaboration is a core principle of Agile methodologies. Teams are typically cross-functional, including developers, testers, designers, and business representatives. This diversity ensures that decisions consider technical feasibility, user experience, and business impact. Agile teams often work closely with stakeholders and customers, incorporating their feedback into the development process. For example, frequent demos and usability testing sessions provide opportunities to validate assumptions and adjust priorities based on real-world feedback.

Agile also emphasizes **incremental delivery**, where teams deliver small, functional pieces of the product rather than waiting until the end of the project to release a complete system. This approach reduces risk by ensuring that users see tangible progress early and often. For example, an e-commerce platform might first release a basic product catalog, followed by features like search functionality, user accounts, and payment processing in subsequent iterations.

Backlog refinement is an ongoing Agile activity where teams review and update the product backlog to ensure it remains aligned with project goals. During these sessions, teams clarify requirements, estimate effort, and prioritize tasks. For example, a task like "Add a search bar" might be broken into smaller tasks, such as designing the UI, implementing the search algorithm, and integrating it with the backend. This preparation ensures that tasks are well-defined and actionable when sprints begin.

Metrics and tools are integral to Agile methodologies. **Velocity** measures the amount of work a team completes during a sprint, providing insights into their capacity and helping with future planning. **Burndown charts** track progress toward sprint goals, showing how much work remains over time. Tools like **Jira**, **Trello**, and **Asana** support Agile workflows by managing backlogs, visualizing tasks, and automating repetitive processes.

Agile methodologies also incorporate **continuous integration and continuous delivery (CI/CD)** practices to streamline development and deployment. CI ensures that changes are integrated into the codebase frequently, with automated tests verifying that new code doesn't break existing functionality. CD extends this by automating the deployment process, enabling teams to release updates quickly and reliably. For example, a CI/CD pipeline might automatically run tests, build the application, and deploy it to a staging environment when new code is pushed to the repository.

Flexibility is a key advantage of Agile. Unlike traditional methodologies, which require detailed plans and rigid timelines, Agile embraces change. Teams can adjust priorities, add new features, or shift focus as project goals evolve. For instance, if market feedback suggests a new feature will drive significant user engagement, it can be added to the backlog and prioritized for the next sprint.

Agile methodologies also improve team morale and productivity by fostering ownership and empowerment. Teams are self-organizing, meaning they decide how to accomplish their work rather than following directives from above. This autonomy encourages accountability and creativity, as team members take pride in delivering high-quality software.

By breaking work into manageable increments, emphasizing collaboration, and focusing on delivering value, Agile methodologies have transformed software development, enabling teams to respond to change and deliver exceptional products efficiently.

CHAPTER 12: HARDWARE DESIGN AND IMPLEMENTATION

Basics of PCB Design

A **printed circuit board (PCB)** is the foundation of most electronic devices. It mechanically supports and electrically connects electronic components using conductive tracks, pads, and other features etched into copper layers. Understanding PCB design is essential for creating reliable, efficient, and manufacturable electronic systems.

The first step in **PCB design** is defining the requirements for the board. This includes determining the size, shape, and functionality of the PCB. For example, a small wearable device might require a compact PCB, while a larger industrial controller could use a multi-layer board with more space for components. The designer also needs to consider power requirements, operating conditions, and the types of components that will be used, such as microcontrollers, sensors, or power regulators.

Next, the designer creates a **schematic diagram**, which is a blueprint of the electronic circuit. The schematic includes all the components, their connections, and annotations like component values or part numbers. For instance, a resistor might be labeled as R1 with a value of 1 kΩ. Software tools like **KiCAD**, **Eagle**, or **Altium Designer** are used to draw schematics, making it easier to organize complex circuits and ensure accuracy.

After completing the schematic, the design moves to the **PCB layout** stage. This involves placing components and routing the connections between them on a virtual board. The software imports the schematic and creates a board outline, showing the designer where to place components. Component placement is critical for both functionality and manufacturability. For example, high-speed components like microprocessors are often placed in the center to minimize trace lengths, while connectors are positioned at the edges for easy access.

Designing the PCB layout requires careful attention to **trace routing**, which involves drawing the paths that connect components electrically. Traces must be wide enough to handle the required current without overheating. For example, a power trace carrying 2 amps might require a width of 1 mm, depending on the copper thickness. Signal traces, such as those connecting a microcontroller to sensors, can be narrower, but they must avoid interference from other signals.

Ground planes and **power planes** are often used in multi-layer PCBs to provide stable power distribution and minimize electrical noise. A ground plane is a large copper layer connected to the ground pin of all components, reducing electromagnetic interference (EMI). Similarly, a power plane delivers consistent voltage to components. These planes also simplify routing by reducing the number of traces needed for power and ground connections.

When designing traces, **impedance control** is crucial for high-speed or high-frequency circuits. Impedance mismatches can cause signal reflections, degrading performance. Designers calculate the impedance of traces based on their width, thickness, and distance from the ground plane. Tools within PCB design software help ensure that critical signals, such as clock lines or data buses, meet impedance requirements.

Via placement is another key aspect of PCB design. Vias are small holes that connect traces between layers in a multi-layer PCB. For example, if a signal trace starts on the top layer and needs to connect to a component on the bottom layer, a via provides the electrical connection. Vias must be carefully placed to avoid overlapping with other traces or components, and their size must be appropriate for the current they carry.

Component footprints, which define the physical dimensions and solder pad locations of components, must match the actual components used. For instance, a surface-mount resistor might have a 0603 footprint, meaning it measures 0.06 inches by 0.03 inches. Designers must verify that the footprints in the PCB layout align with the components chosen during the schematic phase.

Design for manufacturability (DFM) is an essential consideration during PCB design. Manufacturers have specific capabilities and limitations, such as minimum trace widths, spacing between traces, and the smallest drill size for vias. For example, a PCB manufacturer might specify a minimum trace width of 6 mils (0.006 inches) and a minimum via diameter of 10 mils. Ensuring the design meets these constraints prevents production issues and reduces costs.

Thermal management is another critical aspect of PCB design, especially in high-power applications. Heat-generating components, such as power transistors or voltage regulators, need adequate cooling. Designers use thermal vias, heat sinks, or copper pours to dissipate heat effectively. For instance, placing thermal vias beneath a power IC can transfer heat to the bottom layer, where it is dissipated into the environment.

Signal integrity becomes increasingly important as circuits operate at higher frequencies. High-speed signals can suffer from crosstalk, where a signal on one trace induces noise on a nearby trace. To mitigate this, designers maintain a minimum spacing between traces and route critical signals over ground planes to shield them. For example, differential signal pairs, such as those used in USB or Ethernet, are routed in parallel with controlled spacing to maintain their integrity.

Design rule checks (DRC) are automated validations performed by PCB design software to ensure the layout adheres to predefined constraints. These rules check for issues like overlapping traces, unconnected nets, or vias placed too close to components.

Running a DRC before finalizing the design helps identify errors that could compromise the board's functionality or manufacturability.

Once the layout is complete and passes all checks, the design is exported as a set of **Gerber files**, which are the industry-standard format for PCB manufacturing. These files include detailed information about each layer of the PCB, including copper traces, solder masks, and silkscreens. The designer also generates a **Bill of Materials (BOM)**, listing all components required for assembly.

Prototyping is the next step, where the PCB is manufactured and assembled in small quantities for testing. Designers use these prototypes to validate the functionality and identify any issues. For example, if a microcontroller doesn't communicate correctly with a sensor, the team may investigate trace routing or power supply stability. Iterations of the design may be needed to address any problems before moving to full production.

Understanding the basics of PCB design involves not only technical knowledge but also an awareness of practical constraints. From schematic creation to layout and manufacturing, every step must be executed with precision to create reliable and efficient electronic systems.

Interfacing Peripherals with Microprocessors

Interfacing peripherals with microprocessors involves establishing connections between a microprocessor and external devices, enabling them to communicate and work together. Peripherals can range from simple input devices like switches and sensors to complex output devices like displays and actuators. Effective interfacing requires a combination of hardware design and software programming.

The first step in interfacing is understanding the **communication protocols** supported by both the microprocessor and the peripheral. Common protocols include **GPIO (General Purpose Input/Output)**, **UART (Universal Asynchronous Receiver-Transmitter)**, **SPI (Serial Peripheral Interface)**, and **I2C (Inter-Integrated Circuit)**. For example, a temperature sensor might use I2C to send data to the microprocessor, while an OLED display might use SPI for high-speed communication.

GPIO pins are the simplest way to interface peripherals. These pins can be configured as inputs or outputs, depending on the application. For instance, a push button connected to a GPIO pin set as an input allows the microprocessor to detect when the button is pressed. Conversely, setting a GPIO pin as an output lets the microprocessor control devices like LEDs or relays. Pull-up or pull-down resistors are often added to GPIO circuits to ensure stable signal levels when no input is applied.

For data-heavy communication, **UART** is widely used to interface devices like GPS modules, modems, or serial terminals. UART transmits data as asynchronous serial signals, using TX (transmit) and RX (receive) lines. It requires both devices to share the same baud rate, which defines how fast data is sent. For example, a UART connection operating at 9600 baud transmits 9600 bits per second. UART's simplicity makes it suitable for long-distance communication, but its lack of clock synchronization can limit accuracy in noisy environments.

SPI and **I2C** are synchronous communication protocols, meaning they use a clock signal to synchronize data transfer. **SPI** uses separate lines for data input (MISO), data output (MOSI), clock (SCK), and chip select (CS). This allows high-speed, full-duplex communication, making it ideal for interfacing high-performance devices like SD cards or digital-to-analog converters (DACs). **I2C**, on the other hand, uses only two lines: a serial data line (SDA) and a serial clock line (SCL). Multiple peripherals can share the same I2C bus, with each device identified by a unique address. This makes I2C efficient for systems with multiple low-speed devices like sensors and EEPROMs.

To ensure proper interfacing, **voltage compatibility** between the microprocessor and peripheral must be considered. For example, a microprocessor operating at 3.3V may need a level shifter to communicate with a 5V peripheral. Without proper voltage matching, the devices can malfunction or sustain damage. Additionally, adequate power supply and decoupling capacitors are crucial to prevent voltage drops and ensure stable operation.

Interrupt handling is another critical aspect of interfacing peripherals. **Interrupts** allow the microprocessor to respond immediately to events like a button press or data availability, rather than continuously polling the device. For example, a microprocessor interfacing with a motion sensor might use an interrupt to wake up only when motion is detected, saving power in battery-operated systems.

Writing **device drivers** is essential for enabling software control of peripherals. A device driver is a program that abstracts the hardware details, providing a simple interface for the main application. For example, a driver for an LCD display might include functions like `init_display()`, `write_character()`, or `clear_screen()`. These functions hide the complexity of sending low-level commands to the display.

Testing is a key step in peripheral interfacing. Engineers use tools like **logic analyzers** and **oscilloscopes** to monitor signals and debug issues. For example, if an I2C device fails to respond, the logic analyzer can verify whether the correct start condition, address, and data were sent. Similarly, an oscilloscope can help detect voltage fluctuations or noise on signal lines.

Prototyping and Fabrication

Prototyping and fabrication are critical stages in hardware design, transforming concepts into physical, testable products. Prototyping involves building a functional version of the design, often using easily modifiable materials and components, while fabrication focuses on producing the final product at scale with high precision.

The prototyping process typically begins with a **breadboard** or **perfboard**. A breadboard allows engineers to assemble circuits without soldering, using jumper wires and plug-in components to test functionality quickly. For example, a prototype for a temperature monitoring system might include a microcontroller, a temperature sensor, and an LCD display connected on a breadboard to validate the design. While breadboards are convenient for early-stage testing, they are not reliable for long-term use due to loose connections and signal interference.

Once the circuit is validated on a breadboard, the design is moved to a **perfboard** or **stripboard**, where components are soldered for more stable connections. This step is often used for small-scale or one-off prototypes. Engineers ensure neat routing of wires and correct component placement to minimize errors. For instance, soldering an LED in reverse polarity could prevent it from lighting up, highlighting the need for attention to detail.

For complex or high-performance systems, the design transitions to a **custom PCB (Printed Circuit Board)**. Using PCB design software like **KiCAD**, **Altium Designer**, or **Eagle**, engineers create a layout that matches the schematic, defining the placement of components and routing electrical traces. For example, a PCB for a wearable device might integrate a Bluetooth module, a battery management IC, and a microcontroller, arranged to minimize the overall size.

After the PCB layout is finalized, it is sent for fabrication. PCB manufacturers use **Gerber files**, which contain detailed instructions for etching copper layers, drilling holes, and applying solder masks. Manufacturers offer various options, such as single-sided, double-sided, or multi-layer PCBs. For instance, a multi-layer PCB might include separate power and ground planes to improve performance in high-frequency circuits.

Material selection is a key consideration in PCB fabrication. Most PCBs use **FR4**, a fiberglass-reinforced epoxy laminate, for its durability and insulation properties. For specialized applications, such as RF circuits, materials like **Rogers laminates** with lower dielectric losses are used to ensure signal integrity.

The next step in the process is **assembly**, where components are soldered onto the fabricated PCB. This is done using either **through-hole technology (THT)** or **surface-mount technology (SMT)**. THT involves inserting component leads into holes and soldering them on the opposite side, providing strong mechanical bonds. SMT places components directly onto pads on the surface of the board, enabling smaller, more compact designs. For instance, a smartphone PCB primarily uses SMT to fit numerous components into a small footprint.

Automated machines, such as **pick-and-place machines**, are used in large-scale assembly to position components accurately. These machines use vision systems to align components and place them onto the PCB with precision. After placement, the board goes through a **reflow soldering** process, where it is heated to melt solder paste, creating electrical connections. For through-hole components, **wave soldering** is often used.

Testing is a crucial step after assembly. **In-circuit testing (ICT)** checks for short circuits, open circuits, and component values to ensure the board was assembled correctly. **Functional testing** verifies that the board operates as intended, using test rigs or software scripts to simulate real-world conditions. For example, an assembled PCB for a motor controller might be tested by driving an actual motor to verify speed control and safety features.

When defects are found, engineers perform **rework**, which involves desoldering and replacing faulty components. Tools like hot air rework stations and soldering irons enable precise repairs. Rework is more common during prototyping than mass production, as rigorous quality checks reduce defects in fabricated boards.

For low-volume prototypes, manufacturers often use **3D printing** to create custom enclosures and mechanical parts, enabling rapid iteration. A designer building a prototype for a smart home hub might 3D print a case to house the PCB, buttons, and connectors, ensuring it fits together neatly.

Fabrication at scale introduces additional considerations, such as cost optimization and consistency. **Panelization** groups multiple copies of the PCB into a single panel, allowing manufacturers to process several boards simultaneously. This reduces production time and material waste. For example, a 10 cm by 10 cm panel might contain four smaller PCBs arranged for efficient cutting after fabrication.

Prototyping and fabrication are iterative processes. Each cycle provides important insights, helping refine the design and prepare it for production. From initial breadboard testing to polished PCBs, these stages bridge the gap between concept and reality, ensuring the final product is functional, reliable, and ready for deployment.

CHAPTER 13: CYBERSECURITY AND CRYPTOGRAPHY

Principles of Cybersecurity

Cybersecurity is about protecting systems, networks, and data from unauthorized access, theft, or damage. The principles of cybersecurity ensure that information remains secure while systems perform their intended functions. These principles guide the design and implementation of secure systems and help identify vulnerabilities that attackers might exploit.

Confidentiality is the first principle of cybersecurity. It ensures that sensitive information is accessible only to authorized users or systems. This principle is enforced through mechanisms like encryption, access controls, and authentication. Encryption transforms data into an unreadable format using algorithms and keys. For example, when you use a secure website, your browser encrypts the information you send using protocols like SSL/TLS. This ensures that even if someone intercepts the data, they cannot understand it without the decryption key.

Access control restricts who can view or modify data. Techniques like **role-based access control (RBAC)** assign permissions based on user roles within an organization. For instance, a payroll system might allow HR personnel to view and edit employee salaries but restrict other employees from accessing this data. Strong authentication methods, such as multi-factor authentication (MFA), verify a user's identity before granting access. MFA typically combines something the user knows (password), something they have (a phone or token), and something they are (biometric data like fingerprints).

Integrity ensures that information is accurate and has not been altered. It protects data from being tampered with, whether maliciously or accidentally. Cryptographic techniques like hashing verify data integrity. A hash function generates a unique fixed-size string, or hash, based on the input data. If the data changes, even slightly, the hash value changes dramatically. For example, when downloading software, users often check the hash provided by the software developer to ensure the file wasn't corrupted or tampered with during transit.

Systems also enforce integrity through **input validation**. This process ensures that data entered into a system conforms to expected formats and values. For example, a web application that expects a numeric value for age will reject inputs like letters or special characters. This prevents attackers from injecting malicious data, such as SQL injection or cross-site scripting (XSS) payloads, which exploit system vulnerabilities.

Availability ensures that systems and data are accessible when needed. This principle is critical for organizations that rely on continuous access to services, such as hospitals or financial institutions. Availability is supported by redundancy, failover mechanisms, and regular system maintenance. For instance, load balancers distribute traffic across multiple servers to prevent any single server from becoming overwhelmed. Backup systems and disaster recovery plans ensure data can be restored quickly after an outage.

Authentication, Authorization, and Accounting (AAA) are foundational concepts in cybersecurity. **Authentication** verifies the identity of a user or system. Passwords, biometric scans, and digital certificates are common methods. **Authorization** determines what an authenticated user or system can access. For example, a database admin might have full access to all tables, while a data analyst has read-only access. **Accounting**, or auditing, logs user activities to track who accessed what and when. This helps identify suspicious behavior, such as multiple failed login attempts or unauthorized data access.

Least privilege is a principle that limits access rights for users and systems to the minimum necessary to perform their functions. For example, a software developer working on a specific feature might only have access to the codebase related to that feature, not the entire application. Limiting privileges reduces the attack surface, as even if an account is compromised, the potential damage is minimized.

Defense in depth involves layering multiple security measures to protect a system. No single security mechanism is foolproof, so combining several techniques ensures better protection. For example, a secure system might use firewalls to block unauthorized network traffic, intrusion detection systems (IDS) to monitor for suspicious activity, and endpoint protection to secure devices against malware.

Security by design embeds security considerations into the development process rather than treating them as an afterthought. Secure coding practices, threat modeling, and regular security testing are integral parts of this approach. For example, developers might use tools like static code analyzers to identify vulnerabilities such as buffer overflows or improper input sanitization during the coding phase.

Zero Trust Architecture is a modern cybersecurity principle that assumes no user or system is inherently trustworthy, even within the organization's network. It requires continuous verification of identity, device health, and user permissions for every access request. For instance, a zero-trust system might enforce re-authentication when a user switches from one application to another or accesses sensitive data.

Encryption is a cornerstone of cybersecurity, ensuring data remains confidential and secure during storage and transmission. **Symmetric encryption** uses the same key for encryption and decryption, making it faster but requiring secure key sharing. **Asymmetric encryption**, used in public-key cryptography, employs a pair of keys: one public and one private. For example, secure email systems like PGP (Pretty Good

Privacy) use asymmetric encryption to encrypt messages with the recipient's public key, ensuring only they can decrypt it with their private key.

Non-repudiation ensures that the sender of a message or the author of a transaction cannot deny their involvement. Digital signatures provide non-repudiation by combining cryptographic hashing and asymmetric encryption. For example, when signing a document electronically, the signature includes the sender's private key and a hash of the document, proving the sender's identity and confirming the document's integrity.

Physical security is often overlooked but is equally important. Attackers who gain physical access to servers, routers, or storage devices can bypass many digital safeguards. Measures like biometric access controls, surveillance cameras, and secure server rooms ensure that only authorized personnel can access critical hardware.

Incident response is an essential part of cybersecurity. It involves identifying, mitigating, and recovering from security breaches or attacks. An incident response plan outlines the steps to follow when an incident occurs, including isolating affected systems, analyzing the attack vector, and restoring services. For example, if a ransomware attack encrypts an organization's data, the response team might isolate the infected machines, restore data from backups, and investigate how the malware infiltrated the network.

Social engineering attacks, such as phishing, exploit human vulnerabilities rather than technical ones. Educating users to recognize threats, such as suspicious emails or phone calls, is critical. Multi-factor authentication and email filtering tools provide additional protection against these attacks.

Finally, **regular updates and patches** ensure systems remain secure against emerging threats. Software developers release patches to address vulnerabilities discovered after a product's release. For example, applying a security update to a web server might fix a bug that could otherwise allow attackers to execute arbitrary code. Organizations must establish a patch management policy to prioritize and deploy updates promptly.

Encryption Techniques and Algorithms

Encryption is the process of converting plaintext into ciphertext, ensuring that unauthorized parties cannot read the data. It is one of the most effective tools in cybersecurity, securing communication, protecting sensitive information, and maintaining privacy. Encryption relies on algorithms and keys to transform and reverse the data. The strength of encryption lies in both the algorithm used and the key's security.

There are two primary types of encryption techniques: **symmetric encryption** and **asymmetric encryption**. In symmetric encryption, the same key is used for both encryption and decryption. This method is efficient for large datasets because it requires less computational overhead compared to asymmetric encryption. Common symmetric encryption algorithms include **AES (Advanced Encryption Standard)**, **DES (Data Encryption Standard)**, and **Triple DES (3DES)**.

AES is widely considered the gold standard in symmetric encryption. It operates on block sizes of 128 bits, with key sizes of 128, 192, or 256 bits. For example, AES-256 is commonly used in applications where high security is essential, such as encrypting sensitive financial transactions or securing communication in military operations. The encryption process involves multiple rounds of substitution, transposition, and mixing of plaintext and keys, creating strong resistance to attacks.

DES, one of the earlier encryption standards, uses a 56-bit key to encrypt 64-bit blocks of data. While revolutionary in the 1970s, DES is now considered insecure due to its short key length, making it vulnerable to brute-force attacks. **Triple DES** improved upon DES by applying the encryption process three times with different keys, increasing its strength. However, 3DES has also been largely phased out in favor of AES due to its slower performance and the increasing efficiency of modern attacks.

In contrast, **asymmetric encryption** uses a pair of keys: a **public key** for encryption and a **private key** for decryption. This key pair is mathematically linked but ensures that data encrypted with the public key can only be decrypted with the private key, and vice versa. Asymmetric encryption is the foundation of modern cryptography, enabling secure key exchange, digital signatures, and authentication protocols.

RSA (Rivest-Shamir-Adleman) is the most widely used asymmetric encryption algorithm. It relies on the difficulty of factoring large numbers into their prime components, which makes it computationally infeasible to break without the private key. RSA typically uses key sizes of 2048 or 4096 bits, offering robust security. For example, RSA is commonly used in secure email systems, where a sender encrypts messages with the recipient's public key, ensuring only the recipient can decrypt the content with their private key.

Another prominent asymmetric encryption algorithm is **Elliptic Curve Cryptography (ECC)**. ECC provides the same level of security as RSA but with much smaller key sizes. For instance, a 256-bit ECC key is as secure as a 3072-bit RSA key. This makes ECC highly efficient for devices with limited processing power or memory, such as IoT devices and smartphones. ECC is commonly used in applications like SSL/TLS certificates and blockchain systems.

Hybrid encryption combines the benefits of symmetric and asymmetric encryption. In this approach, asymmetric encryption is used to securely exchange a symmetric key, which is then used for encrypting the actual data. This method leverages the speed of symmetric encryption and the security of asymmetric encryption. For instance, in HTTPS (secure web browsing), the SSL/TLS handshake uses asymmetric encryption to exchange a symmetric session key, after which all subsequent communication is encrypted symmetrically.

Encryption algorithms also vary by their mode of operation, especially in block ciphers like AES. The **ECB (Electronic Codebook)** mode encrypts each block of plaintext independently, but this can reveal patterns in the data, making it insecure for most applications. **CBC (Cipher Block Chaining)** mode addresses this by XORing each plaintext block with the previous ciphertext block before encryption, ensuring that identical plaintext blocks produce different ciphertexts.

For more advanced use cases, **GCM (Galois/Counter Mode)** combines encryption with message authentication. GCM provides both data confidentiality and integrity, making it a popular choice in modern protocols like TLS 1.3. By incorporating an authentication tag, GCM ensures that any tampering with the encrypted message is detectable during decryption.

Hashing is another cryptographic technique closely related to encryption, though it serves a different purpose. While encryption is reversible, hashing is a one-way process that generates a fixed-size output, or hash, from input data. Hash functions like **SHA-256 (Secure Hash Algorithm)** are widely used for verifying data integrity. For example, downloading a file from a trusted source often includes a hash value that users can compare to ensure the file wasn't tampered with.

In password security, hashing ensures that even if a database is compromised, attackers cannot easily retrieve the original passwords. Techniques like **salting**—adding random data to the password before hashing—prevent attackers from using precomputed dictionaries of common hashes, known as rainbow tables.

End-to-end encryption (E2EE) is a practical application of encryption that ensures data is encrypted at the sender's end and only decrypted at the recipient's end. Messaging platforms like WhatsApp and Signal implement E2EE, meaning no intermediaries, including the service providers, can access the plaintext messages. This level of security relies on both symmetric and asymmetric encryption, with keys exchanged securely between the communicating parties.

Encryption also underpins **digital signatures**, which provide authenticity and non-repudiation. A digital signature is created by hashing a message and encrypting the hash with the sender's private key. The recipient can decrypt the hash using the sender's public key and compare it to the hash of the received message. If the two match, the message is confirmed to be authentic and untampered.

In **modern cryptographic protocols**, such as **Quantum Key Distribution (QKD)**, encryption is evolving to address emerging threats like quantum computing. Quantum computers have the potential to break existing encryption schemes, such as RSA and ECC, by solving mathematical problems that are currently infeasible. QKD uses the principles of quantum mechanics to securely exchange cryptographic keys, ensuring that any attempt to intercept the key alters its state and alerts the communicating parties.

Encryption techniques also extend to specialized use cases. For example, **homomorphic encryption** allows computations to be performed on encrypted data without decrypting it. This is particularly useful in privacy-sensitive fields like healthcare and finance, where sensitive data must remain encrypted even during processing. For instance, a hospital could outsource computations on patient data to a cloud service without exposing the underlying information.

Despite its strengths, encryption is not infallible and must be implemented correctly. Weak keys, poor random number generators, and improper key management can compromise even the strongest algorithms. For example, reusing encryption keys across multiple sessions increases the risk of key compromise. Effective **key management systems (KMS)** securely generate, distribute, and store cryptographic keys to mitigate these risks.

Threat Detection and Prevention

Threat detection and prevention are essential components of cybersecurity, focused on identifying and mitigating risks to systems, networks, and data. Effective approaches combine tools, strategies, and technologies to address threats at every stage of an attack, from reconnaissance to execution.

The first step in threat detection is **monitoring network traffic** for unusual or suspicious activity. Tools like **Intrusion Detection Systems (IDS)** analyze data packets flowing through a network, looking for patterns that match known attack signatures. For instance, if an IDS detects a high volume of requests to a single server from multiple IP addresses, it might flag this as a potential **Distributed Denial of Service (DDoS)** attack. IDS tools are often paired with **Intrusion Prevention Systems (IPS)**, which go a step further by automatically blocking or mitigating detected threats.

Modern threat detection systems rely heavily on **machine learning and behavioral analysis**. Traditional signature-based detection only identifies known threats, leaving systems vulnerable to new or modified attacks. Machine learning models analyze baseline behaviors for users, devices, and applications, detecting anomalies that might indicate an attack. For example, if an employee's account suddenly starts downloading large amounts of data outside regular working hours, the system could trigger an alert for further investigation.

Endpoint Detection and Response (EDR) tools focus on protecting individual devices, such as laptops, servers, and IoT devices. These tools continuously monitor endpoints for signs of compromise, such as unexpected file modifications, unrecognized processes, or attempts to disable security software. For instance, EDR solutions might flag and isolate a system infected with ransomware before it can encrypt critical files. Advanced EDR tools also support **remote forensics**, allowing security teams to investigate compromised endpoints without disrupting operations.

Threat intelligence enhances detection capabilities by providing up-to-date information about emerging threats, attack methods, and malicious actors. Security teams subscribe to **threat intelligence feeds**, which aggregate data from multiple sources, including past incidents, open-source reports, and private research. For example, a threat feed might include indicators of compromise (IOCs), such as IP addresses, domain names, or file hashes associated with known attacks. By cross-referencing this intelligence with network activity, organizations can identify and block threats before they cause harm.

Preventing threats begins with **perimeter defenses**, such as **firewalls** and **network access controls**. Firewalls inspect incoming and outgoing traffic, enforcing policies to block unauthorized access. Modern firewalls, known as **Next-Generation Firewalls (NGFWs)**, integrate additional features like deep packet inspection, application control, and threat intelligence. For example, an NGFW might prevent malware from communicating with its command-and-control server by blocking traffic to suspicious domains.

Access control mechanisms are equally critical in preventing unauthorized access. **Zero Trust Architecture (ZTA)** assumes that no user or device is inherently trustworthy, requiring continuous authentication and authorization for every action. For instance, a zero-trust system might enforce multi-factor authentication (MFA) for all users and require device health checks before granting access to sensitive resources. This minimizes the impact of compromised credentials, as attackers cannot move freely within the network.

Encryption is another foundational prevention technique, ensuring that intercepted data cannot be read without the proper decryption key. For example, encrypting communications with SSL/TLS protects against **man-in-the-middle (MITM)** attacks, where attackers attempt to intercept or alter data between two parties. Similarly, encrypting sensitive files at rest prevents attackers from accessing the information even if they breach storage systems.

Regular **patch management** is vital for preventing exploitation of software vulnerabilities. Attackers often target outdated systems with known security flaws, such as unpatched operating systems or outdated applications. Organizations must establish patching schedules to apply updates promptly, especially for critical vulnerabilities. For example, failure to patch systems affected by the **EternalBlue exploit** allowed the **WannaCry ransomware** to spread globally in 2017.

Multi-layered defenses, or **defense in depth**, provide redundancy in case one security measure fails. For example, a phishing email that bypasses a spam filter might still be blocked by URL filtering if the recipient clicks on a malicious link. Similarly, endpoint protection software can prevent malware from executing even if it is inadvertently downloaded.

Data Loss Prevention (DLP) tools focus on protecting sensitive information from unauthorized access or exfiltration. These tools monitor data at rest, in transit, and in use, applying rules to prevent leaks. For instance, a DLP system might block an email attachment containing sensitive customer data from being sent to an external address. By enforcing compliance with data protection policies, DLP systems help prevent breaches and ensure regulatory adherence.

Security teams also employ **honeypots** and **honeynets** as proactive detection tools. Honeypots are decoy systems or services designed to attract attackers, diverting them from real targets and gathering intelligence on their methods. For example, a honeypot might simulate a vulnerable database, logging attackers' actions for analysis. Honeynets extend this concept to entire networks of decoys, creating more realistic environments that can capture detailed attack information.

Incident response plans are an essential part of threat prevention. Even the best defenses cannot prevent every attack, so organizations must be prepared to respond quickly and effectively when threats are detected. A well-defined plan includes steps for identifying the attack, containing its spread, eradicating the threat, and recovering systems. For instance, in the event of a ransomware attack, the plan might prioritize isolating infected systems, restoring backups, and identifying the source of the compromise.

Finally, **user education** is one of the most effective prevention strategies. Many attacks, such as phishing and social engineering, exploit human vulnerabilities rather than technical ones. Regular training programs teach employees to recognize suspicious emails, avoid clicking on unverified links, and report potential security incidents. For example, a simulated phishing exercise might help employees identify red flags, such as misspelled domains or urgent requests for sensitive information.

Threat detection and prevention require a holistic approach that combines advanced technology, robust processes, and human awareness.

CHAPTER 14: ARTIFICIAL INTELLIGENCE AND MACHINE LEARNING

Overview of AI and ML

Artificial Intelligence (AI) refers to the development of systems that can perform tasks requiring human intelligence. These tasks include reasoning, learning, problem-solving, perception, and decision-making. **Machine Learning (ML)** is a subset of AI that focuses on building systems that learn and improve from experience without being explicitly programmed. Together, AI and ML are transforming industries, enabling automation, enhancing decision-making, and solving complex problems.

At its core, **AI involves three key components**: data, algorithms, and computing power. Data is the foundation of AI. Systems analyze vast amounts of information to identify patterns, extract insights, and make decisions. Algorithms are the instructions that allow machines to process this data, while computing power provides the resources needed to handle complex computations quickly. For instance, training a neural network to recognize faces requires millions of images, powerful processors, and advanced algorithms.

AI can be classified into **narrow AI, general AI**, and **superintelligent AI**. Narrow AI, also known as weak AI, focuses on specific tasks. Examples include virtual assistants like Siri or Alexa, recommendation systems on Netflix, and spam filters in email. These systems excel in their domains but lack the ability to perform tasks outside their programming. General AI, by contrast, refers to systems with intelligence comparable to humans, capable of reasoning and solving problems across diverse domains. This level of AI remains theoretical, as current technologies are far from achieving it. Superintelligent AI refers to systems that surpass human intelligence, a concept explored mostly in speculative and ethical discussions.

Machine Learning drives many of today's AI applications. ML models learn by identifying patterns in data, improving their performance as they process more information. For example, an ML system trained on customer purchase histories can predict future buying behavior, helping businesses tailor their marketing strategies.

ML can be broadly divided into **three types: supervised learning, unsupervised learning**, and **reinforcement learning**. In supervised learning, models learn from labeled datasets, where the input data comes with corresponding output labels. For instance, a supervised ML model might learn to classify emails as "spam" or "not spam" based on labeled examples. Algorithms like **linear regression**, **logistic regression**, and **neural networks** are commonly used in supervised learning.

Unsupervised learning deals with unlabeled data, where the model identifies patterns and structures without explicit guidance. For example, clustering algorithms like **k-means** can group customers with similar purchasing habits, enabling businesses to design targeted promotions. Dimensionality reduction techniques like **Principal Component Analysis (PCA)** are also part of unsupervised learning, helping simplify complex datasets while retaining important information.

Reinforcement learning is a different approach, where models learn by interacting with an environment and receiving feedback in the form of rewards or penalties. This type of learning is commonly used in gaming AI, robotics, and autonomous systems. For example, Google's **DeepMind AlphaGo** used reinforcement learning to master the game of Go, defeating world champions through strategies learned from millions of games.

AI techniques often rely on specialized ML models, including **decision trees**, **support vector machines (SVMs)**, and **neural networks**. Decision trees split data into branches based on conditions, making them easy to interpret. For instance, a decision tree might predict whether a customer will buy a product by analyzing their age, income, and purchase history. SVMs classify data by finding the optimal boundary between classes, such as distinguishing between images of cats and dogs. Neural networks, inspired by the structure of the human brain, consist of layers of interconnected nodes (neurons) that process data and make predictions.

A particularly powerful type of neural network is the **convolutional neural network (CNN)**, which excels at processing image data. CNNs use convolutional layers to detect features like edges, textures, and shapes in images. They are widely used in applications like facial recognition, medical imaging, and object detection. Another type, the **recurrent neural network (RNN)**, specializes in sequential data like time series or text. RNNs use loops to retain information about previous inputs, making them effective for tasks like speech recognition and natural language processing.

AI systems also use **natural language processing (NLP)** to understand and generate human language. NLP techniques power chatbots, language translation tools, and text summarization systems. For instance, **transformer-based models** like GPT (Generative Pre-trained Transformer) and BERT (Bidirectional Encoder Representations from Transformers) have achieved state-of-the-art performance in tasks like question answering, sentiment analysis, and conversational AI.

AI applications often rely on **big data**, which refers to datasets too large and complex to be processed by traditional methods. For example, self-driving cars collect terabytes of data from sensors, cameras, and lidar systems to navigate their surroundings safely. ML algorithms process this data in real-time to make decisions like braking or lane changing.

Deep learning, a subset of ML, focuses on large neural networks with many layers, often called deep neural networks. These networks learn hierarchical representations of data, where lower layers identify simple patterns, and higher layers recognize more complex structures. For example, in image recognition, early layers might detect edges, while later layers identify objects like cars or trees.

Training deep learning models requires significant computational resources, often provided by **GPUs (Graphics Processing Units)** or **TPUs (Tensor Processing Units)**. These processors are optimized for parallel computations, accelerating tasks like matrix multiplication, which are fundamental to neural network operations.

AI and ML systems also raise challenges, including overfitting, bias, and interpretability. **Overfitting** occurs when a model learns the noise in the training data instead of the underlying patterns, reducing its ability to generalize to new data. Techniques like cross-validation and regularization help mitigate this issue. **Bias** in AI systems reflects the biases present in training data, leading to unfair or inaccurate predictions. For example, a facial recognition system trained primarily on images of light-skinned individuals might perform poorly on darker-skinned individuals. Addressing bias requires diverse datasets and careful evaluation.

Interpretability is another challenge, especially with complex models like deep neural networks. Unlike decision trees, which are easy to understand, deep learning models act as "black boxes," making it difficult to explain their decisions. Researchers use techniques like **SHAP (Shapley Additive Explanations)** and **LIME (Local Interpretable Model-Agnostic Explanations)** to make AI models more transparent.

AI and ML applications span countless industries. In healthcare, AI analyzes medical images for early disease detection, predicts patient outcomes, and suggests personalized treatment plans. In finance, ML algorithms detect fraudulent transactions and forecast market trends. In agriculture, AI systems optimize irrigation schedules, monitor crop health, and predict yields based on weather data.

Despite their transformative potential, AI and ML require careful ethical considerations. Privacy concerns arise when models analyze sensitive data, such as personal health records or browsing histories. Developers must ensure compliance with regulations like GDPR and design systems that respect user privacy.

Neural Networks

Neural networks are computational models inspired by the structure and function of the human brain. They consist of layers of interconnected nodes, or neurons, that process data and make predictions. Each neuron receives inputs, applies a mathematical transformation, and passes the output to other neurons in the network. Neural networks are the foundation of many artificial intelligence (AI) applications, including image recognition, speech processing, and autonomous systems.

A **basic neural network** consists of three types of layers: the **input layer**, **hidden layers**, and the **output layer**. The input layer receives raw data, such as pixel values from an image or numerical features from a dataset. Hidden layers process the data through a series of transformations, extracting patterns and relationships. The output layer produces the final prediction, such as a class label or a numerical value.

Each connection between neurons has an associated weight, which determines the importance of the input in generating the output. For example, in a network recognizing handwritten digits, certain connections might emphasize features like edges or loops. Neurons also include a bias term, which shifts the activation function to improve learning. **Activation functions** introduce non-linearity into the network, enabling it to model complex relationships. Common activation functions include **ReLU (Rectified Linear Unit)**, which outputs the input value for positive inputs and zero for negative inputs, and **sigmoid**, which maps inputs to a range between 0 and 1.

Training a neural network involves adjusting its weights and biases to minimize prediction errors. This process uses a method called **backpropagation**, which calculates the gradient of the error with respect to each weight. The **gradient descent algorithm** updates the weights in the direction that reduces the error. For instance, if a network predicts an image of a "7" as a "1," backpropagation adjusts the weights to correct this mistake during the next iteration.

Neural networks can be categorized based on their architecture. **Feedforward neural networks** are the simplest type, where data flows in one direction from the input to the output. These networks are effective for tasks like regression and classification. **Convolutional Neural Networks (CNNs)**, specialized for image processing, use convolutional layers to detect spatial patterns like edges, textures, and shapes. For sequential data, such as time series or text, **Recurrent Neural Networks (RNNs)** are used. RNNs have feedback loops that allow them to retain information about previous inputs, making them effective for tasks like language translation or speech recognition.

Despite their power, neural networks have limitations. They require large amounts of labeled data to train effectively and are computationally expensive, especially for deep architectures with many layers. Overfitting, where the network memorizes the training data instead of generalizing to new inputs, is another common challenge. Techniques like **dropout**, where random neurons are ignored during training, and **L2 regularization**, which penalizes large weight values, help mitigate overfitting.

Neural networks have revolutionized fields like computer vision, natural language processing, and robotics. They enable self-driving cars to interpret road conditions, power virtual assistants like Siri, and detect diseases from medical scans. As architectures and training methods continue to improve, neural networks remain a cornerstone of artificial intelligence.

Deep Learning Basics

Deep learning is a subset of machine learning that focuses on models with many layers, known as **deep neural networks**. These models excel at extracting complex patterns from large datasets, enabling breakthroughs in areas like image recognition, natural language processing, and reinforcement learning. The depth of a network, or the number of layers, allows it to learn hierarchical representations of data, where lower layers capture simple features and higher layers represent abstract concepts.

Deep learning relies on large amounts of data and significant computational power. For example, training a deep learning model to recognize objects in images requires millions of labeled examples and specialized hardware like **GPUs (Graphics Processing Units)** or **TPUs (Tensor Processing Units)**. These processors are optimized for the matrix operations that underlie neural network computations, enabling faster training and inference.

A fundamental component of deep learning is the **loss function**, which measures how well the model's predictions match the actual outcomes. Common loss functions include **mean squared error** for regression tasks and **cross-entropy loss** for classification tasks. During training, the model minimizes the loss function by adjusting its weights using gradient-based optimization algorithms, such as **stochastic gradient descent (SGD)** or its variants like **Adam**.

Deep learning models also use different types of layers to process data. **Dense layers**, where every neuron is connected to every other neuron in adjacent layers, are standard in feedforward neural networks. **Convolutional layers**, a hallmark of Convolutional Neural Networks (CNNs), use small filters to scan input data for local patterns, making them efficient for image and video analysis. **Recurrent layers**, found in Recurrent Neural Networks (RNNs), include loops that allow the model to process sequential data, like text or audio, by retaining information from previous inputs.

To train deep models effectively, techniques like **batch normalization** and **dropout** are used. Batch normalization normalizes inputs to each layer, reducing internal covariate shift and accelerating training. Dropout randomly disables neurons during training, preventing the model from becoming overly reliant on specific connections and reducing overfitting. These techniques improve the generalization ability of deep learning models.

Deep learning frameworks like **TensorFlow**, **PyTorch**, and **Keras** simplify the development of neural networks. These libraries provide pre-built components, such as layers, optimizers, and loss functions, allowing developers to focus on model design and experimentation. For instance, building a CNN to classify images in PyTorch might involve stacking convolutional, pooling, and dense layers, followed by compiling the model with an appropriate loss function and optimizer.

Applications of deep learning span numerous fields. In healthcare, deep learning models analyze medical images to detect conditions like cancer or diabetic retinopathy with high accuracy. In autonomous driving, deep networks process sensor data to identify objects, predict vehicle trajectories, and make real-time driving decisions. In entertainment, generative models like GANs (Generative Adversarial Networks) create realistic images, videos, and audio, enabling applications like deepfake generation and content creation.

Deep learning also powers advances in **natural language processing (NLP)**. Models like **BERT (Bidirectional Encoder Representations from Transformers)** and **GPT (Generative Pre-trained Transformer)** use attention mechanisms to process text efficiently, enabling applications like machine translation, question answering, and conversational AI. These models have set benchmarks in NLP tasks, transforming how machines understand and generate human language.

While deep learning offers unparalleled capabilities, it also presents challenges. Training deep networks is resource-intensive and time-consuming, often requiring days or weeks for large-scale models. The "black-box" nature of deep learning makes it difficult to interpret how models make decisions, raising concerns about fairness and accountability. Researchers are developing techniques like **SHAP** and **LIME** to improve the interpretability of these models, ensuring they can be trusted in critical applications like healthcare and finance.

Deep learning represents a leap forward in AI, enabling machines to perform tasks once considered exclusive to humans. As algorithms and hardware continue to evolve, deep learning will drive the next generation of intelligent systems.

Applications of AI in Engineering

Artificial Intelligence is revolutionizing engineering by automating complex tasks, optimizing processes, and enabling the design of innovative systems. Across various engineering disciplines, AI applications leverage techniques like machine learning, deep learning, and natural language processing to tackle challenges that were once considered insurmountable.

In **mechanical engineering**, AI enhances product design and prototyping. Traditional design processes rely on iterative testing and manual adjustments, which can be time-consuming and costly. AI-driven **generative design tools**, such as those provided by Autodesk or Siemens, take a different approach. These systems analyze design constraints, such as material strength, weight, and manufacturing methods, and automatically generate multiple optimal solutions. For instance, a designer creating a lightweight aircraft component might input requirements for weight, load-bearing capacity, and aerodynamics. The AI tool produces a range of designs, allowing engineers to choose the best option while reducing material usage and manufacturing time.

Predictive maintenance is another transformative application of AI in mechanical systems. By analyzing sensor data from machinery, AI systems detect patterns that indicate wear and tear or imminent failures. For example, vibration data from a turbine might show anomalies that suggest bearing degradation. Using **machine learning models**, engineers can predict the remaining useful life of the component and schedule repairs before breakdowns occur. This minimizes downtime, reduces costs, and extends the lifespan of critical equipment. Predictive maintenance is widely used in industries such as aerospace, automotive, and manufacturing, where machinery failures can lead to significant losses.

In **civil engineering**, AI is improving the planning and management of large-scale construction projects. **Building Information Modeling (BIM)** platforms integrate AI to optimize construction schedules, material procurement, and resource allocation. AI algorithms analyze project data to identify inefficiencies, prevent delays, and ensure projects stay within budget. For instance, by using drone imagery and AI-powered analytics, project managers can monitor construction progress in real time, comparing actual progress against planned timelines. This enables proactive decision-making, reducing waste and delays.

AI also is important in **structural health monitoring**. Sensors embedded in bridges, skyscrapers, and dams collect data on stress, strain, and vibrations. AI models process this data to detect structural weaknesses or potential failures. For example, an AI system monitoring a suspension bridge might identify unusual stress patterns caused by wind or traffic loads, prompting engineers to conduct inspections and reinforce the structure before significant damage occurs. This approach enhances safety and reduces maintenance costs.

In **electrical engineering**, AI is transforming the design and operation of power systems. **Smart grids** use AI to balance energy supply and demand, integrate renewable energy sources, and reduce outages. By analyzing data from sensors, smart meters, and weather forecasts, AI algorithms optimize the distribution of electricity across the grid. For example, during a heatwave, an AI system might predict increased energy consumption and adjust power generation accordingly to prevent blackouts. Additionally, AI enables real-time fault detection and isolation, ensuring that disruptions in one part of the grid do not affect the entire system.

AI also accelerates the design of **electronic circuits**. Tools like Cadence and Synopsys integrate AI to automate circuit layout, component placement, and routing. These systems analyze design constraints, such as signal integrity and thermal performance, to create optimal layouts. For example, AI-driven Electronic Design Automation (EDA) tools might generate a circuit board layout that minimizes electromagnetic interference in high-frequency devices. This reduces the time and expertise required for complex electronic designs.

In **chemical engineering**, AI improves the efficiency of chemical processes and accelerates the discovery of new materials. **Process optimization** involves using AI to model and simulate chemical reactions, identifying conditions that maximize yield while minimizing energy consumption and waste. For instance, in petroleum refining, AI systems analyze sensor data from distillation columns to adjust operating parameters in real time, improving efficiency and product quality.

Material discovery is another area where AI is making significant contributions. Traditional methods of developing new materials rely on trial and error, which can take years. AI accelerates this process by predicting material properties based on their molecular structure. For example, deep learning models can analyze millions of chemical compounds to identify potential candidates for high-performance batteries or lightweight composites. This approach has been used to develop materials for energy storage, aerospace, and biomedical applications.

In **automotive engineering**, AI is driving advancements in autonomous vehicles. Self-driving cars rely on a combination of sensors, cameras, and AI algorithms to perceive their surroundings, plan routes, and navigate safely. **Computer vision systems**, powered by convolutional neural networks (CNNs), detect objects like pedestrians, vehicles, and traffic signs. Meanwhile, reinforcement learning algorithms help vehicles make real-time decisions, such as when to change lanes or adjust speed. For instance, Tesla's Autopilot system uses AI to analyze sensor data and continuously improve driving performance based on real-world experience.

AI also optimizes manufacturing processes in the automotive industry. **Robotic process automation (RPA)** powered by AI enables assembly lines to adapt dynamically to changes in production requirements. For example, AI-powered robots can identify defects in car parts using visual inspection and adjust their operations to maintain quality standards. Additionally, AI systems optimize supply chain management, predicting demand for specific vehicle models and ensuring the availability of required components.

In **aerospace engineering**, AI is enhancing flight safety and efficiency. **Flight management systems** use AI to optimize flight paths, reducing fuel consumption and emissions. For example, by analyzing real-time weather data, an AI system can suggest alternative routes that avoid turbulence and maximize fuel efficiency. AI also improves aircraft maintenance through predictive analytics. By monitoring data from sensors on engines, landing gear, and other critical systems, AI models identify potential issues before they affect flight operations, ensuring passenger safety and reducing maintenance costs.

AI is also revolutionizing **robotics engineering**, enabling robots to perform tasks that require perception, decision-making, and adaptability. **Collaborative robots (cobots)**, equipped with AI, work alongside humans in manufacturing, healthcare, and logistics. For example, in a warehouse, cobots equipped with computer vision and reinforcement learning navigate the environment, pick items, and deliver them to packing stations. AI-powered robots also are vital in hazardous environments, such as mining or nuclear decommissioning, where human presence is risky.

In **environmental engineering**, AI addresses challenges like pollution control and resource management. AI systems analyze satellite imagery and sensor data to monitor air and water quality, detect pollution sources, and predict environmental changes. For instance, AI models might analyze data from weather stations and industrial facilities to forecast air pollution levels in urban areas. In water resource management, AI optimizes irrigation schedules by analyzing soil moisture, weather forecasts, and crop requirements, reducing water wastage and improving agricultural yields.

AI also supports **energy engineering**, particularly in renewable energy systems. Wind turbines and solar panels generate energy intermittently, depending on weather conditions. AI models predict energy generation based on weather forecasts and optimize storage and distribution. For instance, a wind farm might use AI to adjust turbine angles in real time to maximize energy capture during changing wind conditions. Similarly, AI algorithms manage battery storage systems, ensuring that excess energy is stored efficiently and released when needed.

In **biomedical engineering**, AI enhances diagnostics, treatment planning, and medical imaging. AI-driven systems analyze medical scans to detect diseases like cancer, fractures, or neurological conditions with high accuracy. For example, AI algorithms can identify subtle patterns in MRI scans that may indicate early stages of Alzheimer's disease, enabling timely intervention. AI also supports personalized medicine by analyzing patient data, such as genetic profiles and medical histories, to recommend tailored treatments.

Across all engineering disciplines, AI empowers professionals to tackle complex problems, improve efficiency, and innovate at an unprecedented pace.

CHAPTER 15: EMERGING TECHNOLOGIES IN COMPUTING

Quantum Computing

Quantum computing represents a paradigm shift in computational power and problem-solving capability. Unlike classical computers, which process information using bits that are either 0 or 1, quantum computers use **quantum bits (qubits)**. Qubits exploit the principles of **quantum mechanics**, including **superposition** and **entanglement**, to perform calculations that would take classical computers an impractical amount of time.

Superposition allows qubits to exist in multiple states simultaneously, representing both 0 and 1 at the same time. For example, while a classical bit can encode only one of two possible states at any moment, a single qubit can represent a superposition of these states. This capability grows exponentially with the number of qubits. A quantum system with 10 qubits can represent 2^{10}, or 1,024 states, simultaneously. In practical terms, this means quantum computers can explore multiple solutions to a problem in parallel, dramatically reducing the time required for certain computations.

Entanglement is another key quantum property that links qubits, such that the state of one qubit is dependent on the state of another, regardless of the distance between them. When qubits are entangled, measuring the state of one qubit immediately determines the state of the other. This interconnectedness allows quantum computers to perform coordinated calculations across qubits, enabling the processing of highly complex problems. Entanglement is integral to many quantum algorithms and provides a computational advantage that classical systems cannot achieve.

Quantum gates are the building blocks of quantum circuits, analogous to logic gates in classical computing. These gates manipulate qubits by altering their probability amplitudes and phase. Common quantum gates include the **Hadamard gate**, which creates superposition, and the **CNOT (controlled NOT) gate**, which entangles qubits. By combining gates into circuits, quantum computers execute algorithms to solve specific problems. For instance, **Grover's algorithm** can search unsorted datasets quadratically faster than classical algorithms, and **Shor's algorithm** can factorize large numbers efficiently, threatening current encryption methods.

Quantum computing excels in specific domains where classical computers struggle. **Optimization problems** in fields like logistics, finance, and manufacturing are prime examples. For instance, quantum computers can optimize supply chain routes by evaluating all possible paths simultaneously, identifying the most efficient configuration. Similarly, in portfolio management, quantum algorithms can balance risk and return across numerous financial assets far faster than traditional models.

In **drug discovery**, quantum computers accelerate the simulation of molecular interactions. Classical computers approximate these interactions due to the computational complexity of modeling quantum mechanical systems. Quantum computers, however, simulate these systems directly, leading to accurate predictions of molecular behavior. For example, researchers are exploring quantum algorithms to identify promising drug candidates for diseases like Alzheimer's or cancer, reducing the time and cost of drug development.

Cryptography is another area undergoing transformation with quantum computing. Current encryption methods, such as RSA, rely on the difficulty of factoring large numbers. Shor's algorithm demonstrates that quantum computers can solve this problem exponentially faster than classical methods, rendering many existing encryption protocols vulnerable. This has led to the development of **post-quantum cryptography**, which focuses on creating encryption methods resistant to quantum attacks. Algorithms like lattice-based cryptography are being designed to secure communication in a quantum-enabled world.

Quantum machine learning (QML) is an emerging field that integrates quantum computing with artificial intelligence. QML aims to speed up training and inference for machine learning models by leveraging the parallelism of quantum systems. For example, quantum computers can process large datasets more efficiently, enabling faster feature extraction and dimensionality reduction. Researchers are exploring applications in image recognition, natural language processing, and predictive analytics, where quantum models may offer significant advantages.

Despite its potential, building a practical quantum computer remains a significant challenge. **Quantum decoherence**, the loss of quantum states due to environmental noise, is a major obstacle. Qubits are highly sensitive to their surroundings, and even minor disturbances can corrupt computations. To address this, researchers use **quantum error correction (QEC)** techniques, which encode information redundantly across multiple qubits to detect and correct errors. However, implementing QEC requires additional qubits and increases system complexity.

Another challenge is the physical realization of qubits. Several technologies are competing to create stable and scalable qubits, each with advantages and limitations. **Superconducting qubits**, used by companies like IBM and Google, rely on the flow of current in superconducting circuits. These systems operate at extremely low temperatures, requiring specialized cryogenic equipment. **Trapped ion qubits**, employed by IonQ, use individual ions suspended in electromagnetic fields. These qubits are highly stable but face scalability issues for large systems. **Photonic qubits**, which use photons, offer the advantage of room-temperature operation and long-distance communication but require precise control over light-matter interactions.

Quantum computers also require specialized software and algorithms to harness their capabilities. Quantum programming languages like **Qiskit** (by IBM), **Cirq** (by Google), and **PennyLane** provide frameworks for designing and testing quantum circuits. These languages allow developers to simulate quantum computations on classical machines, enabling algorithm development before running programs on actual quantum hardware. For example, Qiskit provides tools for implementing quantum Fourier transforms or creating quantum neural networks.

Cloud-based quantum computing platforms are making the technology more accessible. Companies like IBM, Google, and Microsoft offer quantum computers via the cloud, allowing researchers, developers, and businesses to experiment with quantum algorithms without owning the hardware. For instance, IBM's **Quantum Experience** provides free access to a limited number of qubits, while advanced services cater to enterprise needs with higher qubit counts and lower error rates.

Quantum computing also raises ethical and societal considerations. The technology's ability to break current encryption methods poses risks to privacy and security. Governments and organizations are racing to prepare for a **post-quantum era**, where new cryptographic standards will ensure data remains protected. Additionally, quantum computing's resource-intensive infrastructure highlights concerns about its environmental impact. Balancing these challenges with the technology's transformative potential requires careful planning and regulation.

In scientific research, quantum computing is unlocking new possibilities. **Material science**, for example, benefits from quantum simulations that model atomic structures and predict material properties. This has implications for creating superconductors, lightweight composites, and energy-efficient materials. Similarly, in **climate modeling**, quantum computers analyze complex interactions in atmospheric systems, improving predictions of weather patterns and climate change impacts.

As quantum computing continues to advance, interdisciplinary collaboration between physicists, computer scientists, and engineers becomes essential. The integration of quantum and classical systems, known as **quantum-classical hybrid computing**, is a promising approach. In these systems, classical computers handle tasks like preprocessing data, while quantum computers focus on the computationally intensive parts. This synergy maximizes the strengths of both technologies.

Quantum computing represents a frontier in computational innovation. While practical, large-scale systems are still in development, the breakthroughs achieved so far underscore the transformative potential of quantum mechanics applied to computing. From solving optimization problems to advancing cryptography and scientific discovery, quantum computing is poised to redefine what is computationally possible.

Edge and Cloud Computing

Edge computing and **cloud computing** are complementary technologies that address the growing demands of data processing, storage, and real-time decision-making. Both are vital in modern computing by enabling scalable, efficient, and distributed systems, each catering to different needs.

Cloud computing provides on-demand access to computing resources such as servers, storage, and databases over the internet. It offers scalability, flexibility, and cost efficiency by eliminating the need for businesses to maintain physical infrastructure. Providers like **AWS**, **Microsoft Azure**, and **Google Cloud** operate massive data centers, hosting services that power everything from web applications to machine learning workloads. For example, a retail business might use a cloud platform to manage its e-commerce site, analyze sales data, and deploy recommendation engines without investing in hardware.

Cloud computing operates on three primary service models: **Infrastructure as a Service (IaaS)**, **Platform as a Service (PaaS)**, and **Software as a Service (SaaS)**. IaaS provides virtualized computing resources like virtual machines and storage. PaaS offers a development environment where developers can build, test, and deploy applications without worrying about underlying infrastructure. SaaS delivers fully managed software applications accessible via web browsers, such as Google Workspace or Salesforce.

Cloud computing also supports **serverless architectures**, where developers focus solely on writing code while the cloud provider handles infrastructure management, scaling, and maintenance. For instance, AWS Lambda allows users to run code in response to events, such as processing customer orders, without provisioning or managing servers. This reduces operational overhead and ensures that resources scale automatically with demand.

While cloud computing excels at centralizing resources, **edge computing** moves data processing closer to where it is generated. This approach reduces latency, minimizes bandwidth usage, and enhances real-time capabilities. For example, a self-driving car relies on edge computing to process sensor data locally, such as detecting pedestrians or obstacles, because sending this data to a distant cloud server would introduce unacceptable delays.

Edge computing is particularly beneficial in scenarios where connectivity is limited or intermittent. Industrial environments, such as oil rigs or remote manufacturing facilities, use edge devices to monitor equipment, detect anomalies, and trigger automated responses. Similarly, healthcare applications, like wearable devices, process vital signs locally to alert users of irregularities without relying on constant cloud connectivity.

The integration of edge and cloud computing enables hybrid architectures, combining the strengths of both. In a **hybrid cloud-edge system**, critical tasks are processed at the edge for speed and reliability, while the cloud handles long-term storage, analytics, and machine learning model updates. For instance, an IoT-enabled smart factory might analyze sensor data locally to ensure machinery operates safely while uploading aggregated data to the cloud for predictive maintenance.

Edge computing relies on specialized hardware and software. **Edge gateways** act as intermediaries between IoT devices and cloud systems, performing preprocessing, protocol translation, and security enforcement. **Edge AI** devices, such as Nvidia Jetson or Google Coral, incorporate AI accelerators to perform real-time inferencing on data. For example, a security camera with an edge AI chip can detect intruders and trigger alarms without sending footage to the cloud.

5G networks further enhance edge computing by providing high-speed, low-latency connectivity. With 5G, edge devices can offload non-critical tasks to nearby servers, creating a distributed edge ecosystem. This is particularly useful in applications like augmented reality (AR) and virtual reality (VR), where immersive experiences require seamless data processing across devices.

Security is a critical consideration in both edge and cloud computing. While cloud providers invest heavily in securing their platforms, edge environments face unique challenges due to their distributed nature. Edge devices are often deployed in unprotected locations, making them vulnerable to physical tampering and cyberattacks. Securing edge systems requires robust authentication, data encryption, and continuous monitoring.

Data sovereignty is another factor driving the adoption of edge computing. Regulations like GDPR mandate that sensitive data remain within specific geographic boundaries. By processing data locally at the edge, organizations can comply with these regulations while still leveraging cloud resources for broader analysis and storage.

Edge and cloud computing are also transforming **content delivery**. Content Delivery Networks (CDNs), such as Akamai or Cloudflare, use edge servers to cache web content closer to users, reducing load times and improving user experience. For example, streaming platforms like Netflix deliver high-definition videos efficiently by storing popular content on edge servers located near end users.

Both edge and cloud computing are foundational to **Industry 4.0**, enabling smart factories, autonomous vehicles, and intelligent transportation systems. Their synergy ensures that computing resources are allocated efficiently, balancing the demands of real-time decision-making with the scalability of centralized processing.

Trends in IoT

The **Internet of Things (IoT)** continues to expand, connecting billions of devices and enabling smarter systems across industries. Emerging trends in IoT reflect advancements in connectivity, data analytics, and integration with other technologies like AI and edge computing.

Massive IoT deployments are becoming more common as costs for sensors and connectivity drop. These deployments often involve thousands or even millions of devices working together in sectors like agriculture, healthcare, and logistics. For example, precision agriculture uses IoT sensors to monitor soil moisture, temperature, and crop health, allowing farmers to optimize irrigation and fertilizer use. Similarly, in logistics, IoT-enabled tracking devices provide real-time updates on the location and condition of shipments.

Low-power wide-area networks (LPWANs) are driving IoT growth, offering long-range connectivity with minimal power consumption. Protocols like **LoRaWAN** and **NB-IoT** enable devices to operate for years on a single battery, making them ideal for applications like environmental monitoring and smart cities. For instance, a smart parking system might use LPWAN to report available spaces without requiring frequent battery replacements.

IoT and AI integration is enhancing the intelligence of connected devices. AI models deployed at the edge enable devices to analyze data locally and make decisions in real time. For example, a smart thermostat might learn a user's preferences and adjust the temperature automatically based on occupancy patterns and weather forecasts. Similarly, in industrial IoT, AI-powered systems detect anomalies in machinery and predict maintenance needs, preventing costly downtime.

5G connectivity is transforming IoT by providing faster data transfer and lower latency. This enables more responsive and interactive applications, such as autonomous drones, telemedicine, and real-time vehicle-to-vehicle communication. For example, in smart transportation systems, 5G allows cars to exchange information about traffic conditions and hazards, improving safety and efficiency.

IoT security is becoming a top priority as the number of connected devices grows. Cyberattacks targeting IoT systems can disrupt critical infrastructure, compromise data privacy, and cause financial losses. Efforts to enhance IoT security include implementing secure boot mechanisms, end-to-end encryption, and network segmentation. For instance, smart home devices like cameras and door locks now incorporate advanced security features to prevent unauthorized access.

Digital twins, virtual replicas of physical assets, are gaining traction in IoT ecosystems. By connecting sensors to their digital counterparts, organizations can monitor and simulate real-world systems in real time. For example, a digital twin of a wind turbine might use IoT data to analyze performance, predict failures, and optimize maintenance schedules. Digital twins are widely used in manufacturing, healthcare, and urban planning.

Interoperability standards are addressing challenges in integrating devices from different manufacturers. Protocols like **Matter**, backed by industry leaders such as Apple, Google, and Amazon, aim to create a unified framework for smart home devices. This ensures that users can seamlessly connect and control devices across ecosystems, enhancing the usability of IoT solutions.

Environmental sustainability is shaping IoT innovation. Energy-efficient devices, powered by renewable energy sources, are reducing the environmental impact of IoT deployments. For instance, solar-powered IoT sensors monitor air and water quality in remote areas without relying on traditional power grids. Additionally, IoT systems optimize resource usage, such as smart grids balancing electricity supply and demand or smart irrigation systems conserving water in agriculture.

IoT is also driving advancements in **wearable technology**, with devices monitoring health metrics like heart rate, sleep patterns, and blood oxygen levels. These wearables provide actionable insights for users and healthcare providers, enabling early intervention and personalized care. For example, IoT-enabled smartwatches can alert users to irregular heart rhythms, prompting medical attention before serious complications arise.

As IoT continues to evolve, its applications are becoming more intelligent, secure, and sustainable. The convergence of IoT with edge computing, 5G, and AI is unlocking new possibilities across industries, reshaping how systems interact and respond to the world around them.

APPENDIX

Terms and Definitions

- **Adiabatic Computing**: A low-power computing approach based on thermodynamic principles.
- **Algorithm**: A step-by-step procedure for solving a problem or performing a task in a finite number of steps.
- **ASIC (Application-Specific Integrated Circuit)**: A custom-built chip designed for a specific application.
- **Bit**: The smallest unit of data in computing, representing a binary value of 0 or 1.
- **Bus**: A communication system that transfers data between components within a computer or between computers.
- **Bus Width**: The number of bits a system can transfer simultaneously.
- **Byte**: A group of 8 bits used to store a single character of data.
- **Cache**: A small, high-speed storage area that temporarily holds frequently accessed data to speed up processing.
- **Central Processing Unit (CPU)**: The primary component of a computer that performs arithmetic, logic, and control operations.
- **Checksum**: A value used to verify the integrity of data during transmission or storage.
- **Chipset**: A collection of integrated circuits on a motherboard that manages data flow between the CPU, memory, and peripherals.
- **Circuit**: A complete path that allows electricity to flow through electronic components.
- **Clock Speed**: The rate at which a CPU executes instructions, measured in hertz (Hz).
- **Cloud Computing**: A model for delivering computing services over the internet.
- **Compiler**: A program that converts high-level code into machine code that can be executed by a computer.
- **Data Structure**: A method of organizing and storing data for efficient access and modification.
- **Digital Signal Processing (DSP)**: The use of mathematical algorithms to process digital signals for applications like audio and video compression.
- **Digital Twin**: A virtual model that mirrors a physical object or system in real time.
- **DRAM (Dynamic RAM)**: A type of RAM that requires regular refreshing to retain data.
- **EEPROM (Electrically Erasable Programmable Read-Only Memory)**: A type of ROM that can be rewritten and erased using electrical signals.
- **Embedded System**: A dedicated computer system integrated into a larger device to perform specific functions.
- **Emulator**: Software or hardware that mimics the functionality of another system.

- **EPROM (Erasable Programmable Read-Only Memory)**: A type of memory that retains data when power is off and can be erased and reprogrammed.
- **Field-Programmable Gate Array (FPGA)**: A reconfigurable integrated circuit used for hardware customization.
- **Firmware**: Software embedded into hardware to provide low-level control.
- **Floating Point Unit (FPU)**: A specialized part of a CPU for handling decimal and real-number arithmetic.
- **Full-Duplex Communication**: A communication method where data flows simultaneously in both directions.
- **Full-Stack Development**: Development that involves both front-end and back-end programming.
- **Hard Drive (HDD)**: A non-volatile storage device that uses magnetic storage to store data.
- **Hash Function**: A mathematical function that converts input data into a fixed-size output for use in data indexing or cryptography.
- **Heatsink**: A passive device that dissipates heat from electronic components, typically the CPU or GPU.
- **Hyperthreading**: A technology that allows a single CPU core to execute multiple threads simultaneously.
- **Integrated Circuit (IC)**: A set of electronic circuits embedded into a small semiconductor chip.
- **Interleaving**: A method of organizing memory to increase speed by splitting data across multiple channels.
- **Interrupt**: A signal sent to the processor to indicate an event that requires immediate attention.
- **Kernel**: The core component of an operating system that manages system resources and hardware communication.
- **Load Balancer**: A system that distributes workloads across multiple servers to improve performance and reliability.
- **Logic Gate**: A basic building block of digital circuits that performs logical operations like AND, OR, and NOT.
- **Machine Code**: Low-level binary code that a computer's CPU can execute directly.
- **Microcontroller**: A compact integrated circuit designed to govern specific operations in embedded systems.
- **Microkernel**: A minimal OS kernel providing basic services, with additional functionality implemented in user space.
- **Microprocessor**: A single-chip CPU used in computers and other electronic devices.
- **Multiplexing**: A technique for transmitting multiple signals over a single channel.
- **Multiprocessing**: The use of two or more CPUs within a single computer system to perform tasks simultaneously.
- **Nanometer (nm)**: A unit of measurement used to describe the size of transistors in CPUs and GPUs.
- **Network Interface Card (NIC)**: A hardware component that connects a computer to a network.

- **Non-Volatile Memory**: A type of memory that retains data even when the power is turned off (e.g., SSDs, flash drives).
- **Open Source**: Software with publicly accessible source code that can be modified and distributed by anyone.
- **Operating System (OS)**: System software that manages hardware, software, and user interactions on a computer.
- **Overclocking**: Increasing a processor's clock speed beyond its default settings to improve performance.
- **Parity Bit**: A bit added to data for error detection during data transmission.
- **Parity Check**: An error detection method using an additional bit to indicate the parity of a data set.
- **Peripheral**: An external device that connects to a computer, such as a printer, keyboard, or mouse.
- **Pipeline**: A technique in CPUs where multiple instructions are processed at different stages simultaneously.
- **Power Supply Unit (PSU)**: A hardware component that converts electrical power into a usable form for the computer.
- **Printed Circuit Board (PCB)**: A board with conductive pathways to connect electronic components.
- **Quantum Computing**: A computing approach that uses quantum-mechanical phenomena to perform operations on data.
- **Random Access Memory (RAM)**: Volatile memory that temporarily stores data for quick access by the CPU.
- **Read-Only Memory (ROM)**: Non-volatile memory containing permanent instructions for booting a computer.
- **Real-Time Operating System (RTOS)**: An OS designed to process data with minimal delay, often used in embedded systems.
- **Register**: A small, fast storage location within the CPU used for temporary data storage during processing.
- **RISC (Reduced Instruction Set Computing)**: A CPU design philosophy focusing on a small, optimized set of instructions.
- **Scalability**: The ability of a system to handle increasing workloads or expand resources efficiently.
- **Schematic Diagram**: A graphical representation of an electronic circuit.
- **Secure Boot**: A security standard ensuring only trusted software loads during the startup process.
- **Solid-State Drive (SSD)**: A storage device that uses flash memory for faster performance than traditional HDDs.
- **Source Code**: Human-readable programming instructions written in a high-level language.
- **System-on-Chip (SoC)**: An integrated circuit that consolidates all components of a computer system.
- **Throughput**: The amount of data processed by a system in a given amount of time.

- **Token Ring**: A network protocol where devices pass a token to control data transmission.
- **Transistor**: A semiconductor device used to amplify or switch electronic signals.
- **Universal Serial Bus (USB)**: A standard for connecting peripherals to computers.
- **Virtual Memory**: A memory management technique that uses a portion of the hard drive as additional RAM.
- **Virtualization**: The creation of virtual versions of resources like servers, storage, or networks.
- **Volatile Memory**: Memory that loses data when power is turned off, such as RAM.
- **Wavelength Division Multiplexing (WDM)**: A technology for increasing bandwidth by sending multiple signals over a single optical fiber.
- **Wi-Fi**: A wireless networking technology that uses radio waves for data transmission.
- **XOR Gate**: A logic gate that outputs true only when its inputs are different.
- **Zener Diode**: A semiconductor device used for voltage regulation in circuits.

Timeline of Computer Engineering

Early Foundations (Pre-1900s)

- **1837**: **Charles Babbage** designs the **Analytical Engine**, the first concept of a general-purpose computer. Though it was never completed, its design included key elements like a central processing unit (the "mill"), memory (the "store"), and input/output.
- **1843**: **Ada Lovelace** publishes notes on Babbage's Analytical Engine, introducing the idea of algorithms for machines, making her the first computer programmer.
- **1854**: **George Boole** publishes "An Investigation of the Laws of Thought," laying the foundation for **Boolean algebra**, which later becomes critical for digital logic design.

1900s to 1940s: Birth of Modern Computing

- **1937**: **Alan Turing** publishes his paper on the **Turing Machine**, a theoretical framework for understanding computation and algorithms.
- **1941**: **Konrad Zuse** builds the **Z3**, the first programmable digital computer.
- **1943**: **Colossus**, the first programmable electronic computer, is developed in the UK for code-breaking during World War II.
- **1945**: **John von Neumann** proposes the **stored-program architecture**, later known as the **von Neumann architecture**, a model used in almost all modern computers.

- **1946**: The **ENIAC (Electronic Numerical Integrator and Computer)**, the first general-purpose electronic digital computer, is completed in the United States.

1950s: Early Transistors and Operating Systems

- **1951**: **UNIVAC I**, the first commercial computer, is delivered to the US Census Bureau.
- **1956**: IBM introduces the **IBM 305 RAMAC**, the first computer with a hard disk drive for storage.
- **1957**: **FORTRAN** (Formula Translation), one of the first high-level programming languages, is developed by IBM.
- **1958**: **Jack Kilby** and **Robert Noyce** independently invent the **integrated circuit (IC)**, revolutionizing electronic design.
- **1959**: **COBOL** (Common Business-Oriented Language), designed for business applications, is created.

1960s: The Mainframe Era

- **1960**: The first **real-time operating system**, the **Compatible Time-Sharing System (CTSS)**, is developed at MIT.
- **1964**: IBM announces the **System/360**, a family of compatible mainframe computers, standardizing hardware and software interfaces.
- **1965**: **Moore's Law** is proposed by Gordon Moore, predicting the doubling of transistors on a chip every two years.
- **1968**: **Douglas Engelbart** demonstrates the first computer mouse during "The Mother of All Demos," showcasing a graphical interface, word processing, and hyperlinks.

1970s: Microprocessors and Personal Computing

- **1971**: Intel releases the **Intel 4004**, the first commercially available microprocessor, marking the beginning of modern microcomputers.
- **1973**: The first **Ethernet network** is developed by **Robert Metcalfe** at Xerox PARC, enabling local area networking.
- **1975**: The **Altair 8800**, an early personal computer, sparks the microcomputer revolution. Bill Gates and Paul Allen write software for it, leading to the founding of Microsoft.
- **1976**: **Apple Computer** is founded by Steve Jobs, Steve Wozniak, and Ronald Wayne. The **Apple I** is released as a kit for hobbyists.
- **1977**: The **Apple II**, one of the first successful mass-produced personal computers, is launched.

- **1978**: The **VAX-11/780** by Digital Equipment Corporation introduces 32-bit computing.

1980s: Graphical Interfaces and Networking

- **1981**: IBM releases the **IBM PC**, establishing a new standard in personal computing.
- **1983**: **ARPANET**, the precursor to the internet, adopts the **TCP/IP protocol suite**, enabling reliable global networking.
- **1984**: Apple launches the **Macintosh**, the first widely available personal computer with a **graphical user interface (GUI)**.
- **1985**: Microsoft releases **Windows 1.0**, introducing a GUI environment for PCs.
- **1989**: **Tim Berners-Lee** proposes the concept of the **World Wide Web**, a system for sharing information across the internet.

1990s: The Internet Boom

- **1991**: The **World Wide Web** goes live, with the first web browser and server developed by Tim Berners-Lee.
- **1993**: **Mosaic**, the first widely used web browser, makes the internet accessible to the general public.
- **1995**: **Java**, a platform-independent programming language, is released by Sun Microsystems, popularizing cross-platform development.
- **1997**: IBM's **Deep Blue** defeats world chess champion Garry Kasparov, marking a milestone in AI.
- **1999**: The term "**Internet of Things (IoT)**" is coined by Kevin Ashton, envisioning a network of interconnected devices.

2000s: Mobile Computing and Cloud Revolution

- **2001**: Apple launches the **iPod**, revolutionizing digital music storage and playback.
- **2004**: Google releases **Gmail**, pioneering large-scale cloud-based email services.
- **2006**: **Amazon Web Services (AWS)** introduces **Elastic Compute Cloud (EC2)**, popularizing **cloud computing**.
- **2007**: Apple unveils the **iPhone**, combining a phone, media player, and internet browser in one device, ushering in the era of **smartphones**.
- **2009**: Bitcoin, the first decentralized cryptocurrency, is introduced by the pseudonymous **Satoshi Nakamoto**, based on **blockchain technology**.

2010s: AI, Big Data, and Quantum Computing

- **2011**: IBM's **Watson** wins the quiz show **Jeopardy!**, demonstrating advanced natural language processing.
- **2012**: The concept of **deep learning** gains traction with the success of AlexNet, a convolutional neural network, in the ImageNet competition.
- **2014**: **Google DeepMind's** system learns to play Atari games, showing the potential of reinforcement learning.
- **2016**: **AlphaGo**, developed by Google DeepMind, defeats the world champion in Go, a game considered far more complex than chess.
- **2017**: **TensorFlow**, an open-source AI framework, becomes the standard for machine learning research and application.
- **2019**: Google achieves **quantum supremacy** with its quantum computer, solving a problem in seconds that would take classical computers thousands of years.

2020s: Emerging Technologies and Sustainability

- **2020**: The global adoption of **remote work** accelerates due to the COVID-19 pandemic, driving innovation in **cloud computing** and collaboration tools.
- **2021**: Advances in **5G networks** enable faster, more reliable connectivity, supporting IoT and edge computing applications.
- **2022**: Generative AI tools like **ChatGPT** and **DALL-E** demonstrate AI's creative potential in natural language processing and image generation.
- **2023**: Breakthroughs in **neuromorphic computing** simulate human brain functions, paving the way for more energy-efficient AI systems.
- **2024**: Research in **quantum error correction** achieves significant milestones, bringing practical quantum computing closer to reality.

Computer engineering continues to evolve, with ongoing advancements in AI, quantum computing, and edge technologies shaping the future. Each milestone builds on centuries of innovation, pushing the boundaries of what machines can achieve.

AFTERWORD

Thank you for taking the time to journey through *Computer Engineering Step by Step*. Whether you're just beginning to explore this fascinating field or seeking to deepen your understanding, I hope this book has provided you with a strong foundation and sparked your curiosity about the endless possibilities in computer engineering.

Throughout these chapters, we've covered a wide range of topics—from the fundamental building blocks of binary systems and logic gates to advanced concepts like artificial intelligence and emerging technologies. Along the way, we've explored how hardware and software interact, how computers process and store information, and how these systems are designed to solve complex problems. More importantly, we've glimpsed the profound impact computer engineering has on our daily lives and the world at large.

Computer engineering is a field that never stands still. As you read this, new discoveries are being made, innovative designs are being developed, and technology continues to reshape industries and societies. The knowledge you've gained here is not an end point —it's a launchpad. Use it as a starting place to go deeper into the areas that excite you the most, whether that's hardware design, software engineering, cybersecurity, artificial intelligence, or any of the countless other specialties within this vibrant discipline.

This book was designed to break down complex concepts into approachable steps, but it's just one piece of a much larger puzzle. If you find yourself curious about a particular topic, don't stop here. Explore further. Build projects, take courses, collaborate with others, and don't be afraid to experiment. Some of the most valuable learning in computer engineering comes from tackling challenges hands-on and figuring things out as you go.

I'd also like to leave you with one important reminder: computer engineering is as much about creativity as it is about technical skills. At its heart, this field is about solving problems and imagining new possibilities. The tools and principles you've learned here are the foundation, but it's your curiosity, persistence, and imagination that will drive you to innovate and make a meaningful impact.

As you move forward, remember that every step you take builds on the last, and every effort you make contributes to your growth. The path into computer engineering is exciting, challenging, and rewarding, and you are now equipped to take it one step at a time.

Thank you for allowing this book to be part of your learning experience. The future of computer engineering is yours to create. Good luck, and happy exploring!

Made in United States
Troutdale, OR
01/10/2025

27808382R00096